Saint Joseph

People's
Catechism

" . . . *every scribe who is learned in the reign
of God is like the head of a household who
can bring from his storeroom both the new
and the old.*" — Mt 13:52

"*Once you were no people, but now you are God's people*" (1 Pt 2:10).

Saint Joseph

People's Catechism

**A CONCISE CATECHISM OF THE
CATHOLIC FAITH
THAT ANSWERS THE NEEDS
OF PEOPLE TODAY**

By

JOHN R. KLOPKE, C.PP.S.

With added Quotations from the
National Catechetical Directory
"Sharing the Light of Faith"

Illustrated

CATHOLIC BOOK PUBLISHING CO.
NEW YORK

Dedicated to

SAINT JOSEPH

Patron of the Universal Church

Imprimi Potest: Marvin J. Steffes, C.PP.S.
Provincial Director, Province of the Pacific

Nihil Obstat: Richard T. Adams, M.A.
Censor Librorum

Imprimatur: ✠ Joseph T. O'Keefe
Vicar General, Archdiocese of New York

The Bible quotations contained herein are reproduced with permission from *The New American Bible,* Copyright © 1970 by the Confraternity of Christian Doctrine, Washington, D.C. All rights reserved.

Symbolic liturgical illustrations by Anton Manche.

"Excerpts from *Sharing the Light of Faith,* National Catechetical Directory for Catholics of the United States, copyright © 1979, by the United States Catholic Conference, Department of Education, Washington, D.C., are used by permission of copyright owner. All rights reserved."

PHOTO CREDITS: Authenticated News International: 178; Catholic Book Publishing Co.: 150; Ewing Galloway: 2, 26; Glenmary Fathers: 92, 104; Holiday Inn: 170; National Catholic News Service: 61, 69, 75, 120, 134, 137, 142; Matson Photo Service: 10; Religious News Service: 17, 68, 86, 95, 100, 116, 118; Rev. Fred Schroeder: 126; Wide World Photos: 162.

FOREWORD

ACATECHISM is a book; a catechumenate is an experience. The one can never do for the other. Whether or not the formal catechumenate, marked by the Passover experience of Lent and Easter, can ever be adapted to the circumstances of American life and character, it still remains true that no book can substitute for the initiation to Catholicism wittingly or unwittingly provided by a Catholic parish and its pastoral ministry.

This book grew precisely out of such roots. It all began with what looked like a simple question about confession. It grew into a set of classes in what superficially looked like adult education. It ended in an examination of what the Church was meant to be.

Whether all this amounted to the full experience of coming-to-life in Christ is known but to those who shared of themselves with the ostensible instructor. Here are the fruits of it all. Of course, the trunk and branches of the Vine are missing; that is what a catechumenate provides.

J.R.K.

CONTENTS

The land of the Bible.

Chapter 1

THE GOD OF THE BIBLE

1. What do we mean when we call something "divine" or a "god"?

A divine being is something totally *other* than the physical things we experience. It is everlasting, unlimited, and powerful. A divine person or god is thought of as all-knowing, wise, good, and just. Many passages in the Bible express these characteristics of divinity, especially the psalms.

2. Where did people get the notion of "divinity"?

The idea of "gods" arose when people discovered that the world had a regular pattern within which human life could be lived. The gods were thought of as the powerful guardians of the order of the universe.

3. Did people just naturally think that the gods were persons?

No, some peoples never thought that the divinity had any personal characteristics. The poets who wrote the ancient myths seem to have originated the idea that the gods were persons deserving of worship.

4.   In the light of modern science, shouldn't these rather primitive religious ideas be discarded?

In their original form, the notions are indeed primitive. But what the ancient peoples discerned is still meaningful today. There are questions about the universe and human life which lie outside the methods of science.

5.   What question about the universe lies outside the methods of science?

The puzzling question about the universe is why process always brings about an orderly result. Process or change is the *dis*integration of something. Yet the result of process is always the *re*integration of matter into something else. The puzzle is why change shouldn't keep on going until total chaos results. Thus, the ancient idea that there exists some sort of guardian(s) of the world-order is not quite as primitive as it first seems.

6.   What question about the meaning of human life lies outside the methods of science?

The real puzzle is the *source* of the wisdom common to all religions. Even from what we know today about the human mind, it is difficult to trace all religious insight to man's consciousness. Thus, the claim of the ancient myths that there are personal powers higher than man cannot be discounted.

THE SELF-REVEALING GOD OF THE BIBLE

7.   Does the Bible contain all these notions about religion?

Yes, it does. The Bible speaks of a God who is master of the universe and who demands humanity's worship. But the central teaching of the Bible about God is quite different.

8.   What is the central teaching of the Bible about God?

The Bible records a *self-revealing* of God. The Bible speaks of a God who wills to become familiar to humanity instead of being the remote object of its awe and worship. The God of the Bible chooses to take a hand in human history and to direct human life toward purposes altogether surprising and unexpected.

9. Is the notion of a self-revealing of God unique to the Bible?

Yes, it is. Every religion which believes in a self-revealing of God counts the Old Testament of Judaism as part of its faith. It is only there that this notion of God is found. Christianity, for instance, worships the same God as Judaism. But Christianity believes that God's self-revelation became complete in the teachings of Jesus Christ.

GOD REVEALED BY JESUS

10. What is the final self-revelation of God as taught by Jesus?

Jesus speaks of God as his heavenly *Father,* whom he knows intimately and who has sent him to carry out his will. The heavenly Father's will is that all humankind enter into the kingdom of God. It is Jesus' task to establish the kingdom.

11. What is the kingdom of God about which Jesus teaches?

To his Jewish hearers, Jesus' expression "kingdom of God" meant the decisive act of God which would vindicate forever the faith and life of Israel before the pagan world. As Jesus' teaching develops, it becomes evident that God's decisive act is to share his fatherly intimacy and love with those who become Jesus' disciples.

The kingdom is a transformation of human life, beginning with faith and culminating in personal resurrection. This transformation accomplishes the Father's final will to enter into a personal communion with the human race. This is the altogether wondrous goal of human history: God and humankind together in a shared life.

12. Doesn't this make everything in Christianity depend upon the credibility of Jesus?

Yes, it does. The claim of Jesus to know God personally needs to be examined carefully. The gospels present Jesus as one who taught and acted with an authority no prophet ever claimed. The evidence of that authority in the wisdom of his words and the power of his deeds poses the root question of Christianity: just *who* is Jesus?

THE HOLY TRINITY

13. Does Jesus' claim of personal knowledge of the heavenly Father mean that Jesus himself is divine?

Yes, Jesus is truly a divine person. Every Christian creed states that Jesus is truly the eternal Son of God, fully communicating in the Father's divinity. However, Jesus carefully distinguishes himself as a *person* from the heavenly Father. Jesus and the Father are not interchangeable manifestations of a single divinity.

14. Don't Christian creeds state that there is also a third divine person, the Holy Spirit?

Yes, the Holy Spirit is a third divine person. Jesus speaks of someone else who shares fully in the knowledge and love existing between him and the heavenly Father. The personality of the Holy Spirit is mysterious and obscure. But the distinct existence of this divine person is clearly witnessed in the New Testament, especially in the Acts of the Apostles.

One God in Three Persons.

15. How many Gods are there? Three or one?

There is but one divinity fully communicated by the heavenly Father to the Son and, in turn, communicated by Father and Son to the Holy Spirit. This is the doctrine of the Blessed Trinity. The doctrine is derived from the total *unity* of understanding, love, will, and purpose which Jesus shows to exist between himself and the heavenly Father in the Holy Spirit.

As the New Testament explicates this communion-in-divinity, the specific relationships of Father, Son, and Holy Spirit become apparent. We shall explore them in the following questions.

16. When I pray to God, to whom am I praying?

It all depends. There is always a feeling of reverence and worship addressed generally to the divinity in any prayer. This awe in the presence of divinity is addressed equally to all three divine persons. It is a prayer addressed to "God" in the sense of "the divinity." But the prayer does not *name* anyone. If the irreverence be pardoned, such a prayer is like mail addressed to "occupant."

17. When I mean to "name" someone in my prayer to God, to whom am I praying?

Strange as it may seem, you are praying to the heavenly Father. The word "God" as naming someone always means the heavenly Father throughout the New Testament.

18. But if "God" is the special name of the heavenly Father, doesn't it seem that there is something special about his divinity?

If you mean that the Father is, somehow, *more* divine than the Son or the Holy Spirit, you have made a serious error. Father and Son and Holy Spirit each fully communicates in one divinity. In fact the Father wouldn't *be* who he is without everlastingly communicating his full divinity to the Son.

"Father" is who he is. That is his name, not something incidental to who he really is. The same holds true of Father and Son relative to the Holy Spirit. Neither would *be* who he is without the Father with (or through) the Son communicating his full divinity to the Holy Spirit.

The intimacy of incomprehensible understanding and love between Father and Son which *is* the Holy Spirit defines who they are to each other. Their *names* are Father and Son; without the everlasting Spirit uniting them, their relation would be incidental.

Contrast this with human relationships: A man is someone before he becomes a father. Likewise, the relationship of intimacy he has with his son can well be an on-and-off affair. Neither a human father nor a human son is constituted in his very *personality* by his relationship to the other.

19.   What, then, is special about the heavenly Father if prayers which name God are actually prayers to him?

It is the *person* of the heavenly Father which is "special." The same holds true of the persons of the Son and the Holy Spirit. There is something special about them, too. Our prayers may not disregard the real diversity among the persons of the Trinity. We learn of this diversity from Jesus.

20.   What do we learn of the diversity of the persons of the Trinity from Jesus?

Jesus always speaks of himself as sent to do the Father's will, a Father whom he truly loves and obeys. Thus, it would seem that the Father's person is august and majestic. As far as the Holy Spirit is concerned, Jesus always speaks in terms of hidden consolation and holiness. Thus, it would seem that the Spirit's person is self-effacing and inward-turned. As far as Jesus himself is concerned, his words and deeds reveal a person who is loving and responsive.

21.   Does this mean, then, that Christian prayer is never addressed directly to anyone but the august and majestic Father?

The *tendency* is to address all prayer to the Father's august majesty. *Liturgical* prayer is almost always addressed to the Father through the Son in the Holy Spirit. By such prayer we acknowledge the presence of the Spirit inspiring us to pray and we also acknowledge that our prayer would be valueless except for the love the Father has for his eternal Son.

22.   What does this way of praying reveal about Christian belief?

Christian prayer exhibits something more than a general awe and reverence in the presence of the divinity. A Christian stands in awe at the fact that each person of the Trinity has a role to play in his salvation.

23.   Does this mean that the Father, the Son, and the Holy Spirit have different roles to play in my salvation?

As the New Testament describes. it, each person of the Trinity plays his proper role in humankind's salvation. Obvious-

"God's holy people is united in prayer . . . in a common liturgical service, especially the Eucharist" (Vat. II: On Liturgy, no. 41).

ly, the three divine persons act with a unity of understanding and purpose incomprehensible to our divided sort of personality. But each divine person is the focal point of the divine power because of *who* that person is.

The august and majestic Father initiates the divine action in human history. The loving and responsive Son accomplishes our actual salvation. The self-effacing and contemplative Spirit carries on our inward sanctification. If the divine action were carried out differently, the persons of the Trinity would, so to speak, be totally out of character.

24. Wouldn't one ever pray directly to the Son or the Holy Spirit?

It all depends. If this means that Christian prayer should give "equal time" to each of the persons of the Trinity, one really would not be respecting them for *who* they are. We certainly would not address a lengthy and formal speech to a self-effacing friend. So, too, prayer to the Holy Spirit is always a brief and grateful acknowledgment of his presence.

Likewise, we would never put one of our friends center-stage when someone he thinks the world of is present. So, too, prayer to the Son is always directed to what we need to stand in the Father's love. It remains always the Father's august majesty to which we address the praise and dedication and petition of the sort of prayer which Jesus taught his disciples.

25. Does this mean that the persons of the Trinity have truly personal relationships of self-fulfillment something like the self-fulfillment that human persons find in the company of other persons?

Yes, it does. But the question puts it backward. It is human fulfillment which is "something like" the divine self-fulfillment of the persons of the Trinity. Most religions rather naturally suppose that the divinity is *happy*. Only Christianity suggests why this is so. One clue to the inner life of the Trinity is the joy and sense of security which breaks out when Jesus prays to the Father "in the Spirit." (See John, chapter 17, for an example.)

ETERNAL LIFE

26. Is it some share in this inner life of the Trinity which Jesus proclaims as the "kingdom of God"?

Yes, it is. Jesus is not merely inviting us to understand God more deeply or to worship him more sincerely. Jesus is inviting us to experience the self-fulfillment of the three divine persons as they commune in the one divinity.

27. How does Jesus describe this share in the very life of the Trinity?

Jesus speaks of the "eternal life" which he has come to bestow upon his disciples. He is speaking of a totally transformed human existence.

28. Is eternal life the same as heaven?

Not exactly. Many religions have the idea of a heaven in which goodness is rewarded. Christians have the same belief. But the notion of heaven does not occupy a central place in Christian thought. Even the notion of man's immortal soul is not found in the New Testament. It was borrowed from Greek philosophy as a *reasonable* explanation of survival after death.

The earliest Christians simply believed that those who had "died in the Lord (Jesus)" were safe with the Lord until he would return to inaugurate the final and everlasting age of human existence.

29. Does eternal life have different stages to it than just heaven?

Yes, it does. Eternal life begins *now* for one who becomes Jesus' disciple, continues in heaven, and is perfected when Jesus returns for the last judgment. The transformation of human existence proclaimed by Jesus begins with faith, is assured in the experience of heaven, and is completed by an unimaginable expansion of the human person in resurrection to a totally glorious universe. Each stage of eternal life brings a human person closer and closer to the experience which Jesus, the risen Savior, has of the heavenly Father in the Holy Spirit.

GRACE

30. Granting that I believe in Jesus, what does eternal life accomplish in me now?

The very fact that you do have faith in Jesus shows that you have begun a new and wondrous *relationship* to the divine life of the Trinity. This relationship is created in you by an act of sheer graciousness on the part of the heavenly Father. This graciousness is won for you by the saving actions of Jesus as he was gifted by the Holy Spirit. The correct name for this relationship acknowledges the divine graciousness. It is called *grace*.

31. How does grace transform me now?

Grace, first of all, *sanctifies* a believer. Freed from sin, the believer is *empowered* in mind, will, and feelings to live a Christian life. So empowered, the believer is endowed with strength of character to *actualize* in daily life his commitment to be a Christian and to overcome his lapses in Christian duty. In a word, the believer begins to live and act according to the pattern of Jesus. This is where his relationship to the Trinity begins.

32.   What must I do to become a disciple of Jesus?

The Bible says: "Faith comes by hearing." The Christian religion is a *message* which must be taught just as Jesus personally taught the first disciples. This teaching of discipleship is one of the important functions of the Church. Thus, Christian discipleship and church-going are inseparable for one who believes in Jesus.

Chapter 2

GOD AND MAN

CHRISTIAN DISCIPLESHIP

33. Couldn't a disciple of Jesus just read the Bible privately and learn all there is to know about Jesus' teachings?

No, he could not. The Bible is not understandable apart from the Christian community which has pondered and lived its message down through the centuries. The Bible is not a book of philosophy which merely needs to be logically comprehended in order to be understood. The Bible, on the contrary, is a *record* of humankind's experience of God's self-revelation. The record and the community which produced and lives its message are inseparable.

34. Does this mean that one should not read the Bible privately at all?

Obviously, it does not. It means that the Bible should be personally read and pondered in the light of one's experience of a Christian Church. The Church should manifest the Bible's message to an inquirer by its beliefs and life. Of course, if it does not, then the inquirer should turn to another Church.

HOW GENESIS 1—11 WAS WRITTEN

35. Where do I begin my study of God's self-revelation?

One begins with the first book of the Bible, the book of Genesis. The first eleven chapters of Genesis are a kind of prologue which sets the stage for God's intervention in history.

They tell of the creation of the world and humankind's place in it. They then tell of man's sin and degeneration.

36. Are the first eleven chapters of Genesis the most ancient part of the Bible?

No, they are not. What first came to be fixed in the record were the great events which shaped Israel's history, especially the exodus from Egypt. Then, as Israel became acquainted with the records of its pagan neighbors, the need became apparent for an introductory story of "how it all began," such as the pagan myths told.

37. What is so important about the first eleven chapters of Genesis?

These chapters tell us what humanity could have become and what it actually did become. The picture of the world and of humanity presented in these chapters is unique in the history of religion. Then, in chapter twelve, is recorded God's first self-revelation in his calling of Abraham.

38. Where did the materials for the first eleven chapters of Genesis come from?

The were simply borrowed and adapted from ancient Semitic traditions and tales. The chapters *illustrate* how man came to need God's saving action. These chapters are a work of real artistry. The artistry must be appreciated if we are to understand their religious message.

39. Aren't the first eleven chapters of Genesis an historical record of what happened during and after the world's creation?

No, they are not. The author has no special knowledge of world history until he comes to the call of Abraham. In fact, we can identify some of his borrowings from ancient myths. What the first eleven chapters of Genesis do is picture by means of extremely ancient symbols "how it all began."

Whether, for instance, the author actually believed that the world began by a process of differentiation is irrelevant— the belief was common in all the ancient myths and seemed to fit the facts as the ancients knew them. What is relevant is the unique *use*, the artistry with which myth, tale, and legend convey the religious message of Genesis.

CREATION OF THE WORLD

40. Could you give an example of the artistry of the author of Genesis?

For instance, in his account of the origin of the world, the author borrows the idea of *differentiation* from ancient myths. The myths picture the world as coming into being by a process of "sorting out" occurring in an original chaos. One by one, the familiar features of the world appeared: Day-from-night, earth-from-heavens, land-from-sea, sun-from-moon, bird-from-fish, man-from-beast.

But to this tale the author ties the seven-day week which is not in the myths. These are just seven ordinary days, the first of all the weeks of time. His religious message is obvious: In a world where unremitting toil for man and beast was the rule, the author of Genesis strikes a blow for freedom and rest on the seventh day in the name of God.

41. Could you give another example of the author's artistry?

An interesting example is what the author leaves out of the familiar tale. All the myths tell of the *strife* between the gods at the world's beginning. The gods quarrel, their work is difficult, and the results are far from perfect. But nothing of this is recorded in Genesis. Everything appears effortlessly and perfectly at the mere word of God.

The religious message is evident: The one God is better than the whole host of pagan gods. More deeply, the author is teaching that no natural power need be feared or reverenced by man. All things in the universe are but man's fellow-creatures.

42. Does the author of Genesis teach that the world was created from nothing?

No. The technical notion of God as causing the very *existence* of things would have been beyond him. But later biblical authors were not slow to draw this obvious conclusion from the way Genesis pictures everything as appearing by the mere word of God.

MAN, THE IMAGE OF GOD

43. Where did the author get his account of the origin of humankind?

Strangely enough, the account of man's origin is not borrowed from any Semitic tale or myth of which we know. In fact, the ones we do know are rather cynical about humanity, making man an afterthought of the gods. The author of Genesis has no such cynicism. For him, humankind is the crown and lord of creation.

44. How does the author of Genesis teach the dignity of humankind?

There are two lines of teaching about humankind in Genesis. The first account of man's creation (1:26—2:4) emphasizes that man is the very *image* of God. The second account of man's creation (2:5-25) emphasizes the *gifts* bestowed upon the first human couple.

45. Just what is the "image" of God according to which humankind is made?

It is the *dominion* which God bestows upon man that constitutes a true likeness between man and God. Human beings are masters over God's work and, even more, are given the task of improving upon it. The notion that human beings are free and responsible under God is unique to Genesis.

46. Just what is it about human beings which makes them God's image?

This question would have been too philosophical for the author of Genesis. It was not until Jewish thought came into contact with Greek philosophy's notion of "soul" that a reasoned-out explanation became possible. It is the breadth of human intelligence and freedom of human decision which equip man uniquely to deal with the world. These are qualities of the human soul which, as the Greeks discerned, was imperishable.

47. Doesn't the Bible itself teach that man has an immortal soul?

No, it does not. "Immortal soul" is a notion taken from Greek philosophy. What is religiously important in both Judaism and Christianity is God's sheer graciousness in saving *man*, body and soul, from sin and its terrifying consequences. The sinner, immortal soul and all, misses out on God's graciousness.

ADAM AND EVE

48. What are the main features of the second creation-account in Genesis?

The second creation-account teaches a special intervention of God in the creation of each of the sexes. Here we get the names Adam (man) and Eve (one who bears life), the tree, the serpent, and the original sin. The second creation-account is full of symbolism which must be understood if its religious message is to be grasped. Some of the symbols are so ancient that their full meaning is uncertain. But some fairly obvious interpretations can be made of most of them.

49. What do the main symbols of the second creation-account mean?

a) God forms the man from dust and breathes life into him - The man comes from earth like all else but the life-force of man is different.

b) God plants the garden of Eden - The man is made to enjoy an ideal existence.

c) The prohibition to eat of the fruit - The man is morally dependent upon God and not a law unto himself.

d) God creates the animals and man names them - The man has knowledge and power over creation.

e) God creates Eve from Adam's rib - The woman is not an inferior to man but his complement and partner in marriage.

f) The tempter-serpent - An ancient sexual symbol used here to signify total degeneracy.

g) The eating of the forbidden fruit - The decision of the man and the woman to use dominion as if it were owed to no one but themselves.

h) The realization of nakedness - The first experience of the reality and power of evil.

i) The curse put upon the serpent - The struggle of humankind with evil and the promise that it (or a given person) will triumph over evil.

j) The curse on the man and the woman - The introduction of physical and mental anguish, as well as death, into the world.

k) The expulsion from the garden - The rupture of familiar relations between humankind and God.

50. Beneath all the symbols, what is the author of Genesis teaching?

He is teaching that the man and the woman were uniquely *gifted* with moral and physical capacities. These capacities fitted them to live a full and creative existence in companionship and love, each with the other. They were destined to be immortal father and mother of an immortal race. He is teaching that the original sin seriously impaired these capacities and immortality was lost.

"You will be like gods . . ." (Gn 3:5).

SIN AND SATAN

51. Just what was the original sin which affects the whole human race?

It is difficult to say whether the author actually has a specific sin in mind. In fact, the account is so highly symbolized that it is difficult to say what specific event the author has in mind. The symbols he uses point to the heart of *all* sin: the demonic urge to be a law unto oneself. That is what interiorly affects humankind and, through it, the whole world.

52. If God made all things good, where does the tempter-serpent come from?

The serpent personifies something, even somebody, of immense evil force. Its origin is simply not commented on in Genesis. The notion of Satan, God's adversary, appears only later in the Bible.

53. Doesn't the Bible tell of the creation of angels and how some of them sinned and became devils?

The Bible has nothing detailed to say about the origin of angels and demons. In various books of the Bible angelic and demonic forces clash, angels are assigned to guard specific individuals or nations, and angels appear in order to bring God's word to various persons. The world of spiritual forces is simply, somehow, *there* and, at times, impinges upon human affairs. Beyond that, the Bible offers no comment upon its existence.

54. Just who is Satan? Is he a fallen angel or what?

Satan is God's adversary, doomed to failure in all his schemes. Satan is *the* sinner, totally obsessed with being a law unto himself. Various places in the Bible identify him as the leader of the universal forces of evil. "Fallen angel" is surely an apt description of Satan. But how or why he fell, we do not know.

GENESIS AND EVOLUTION

55. How do the creation-accounts of Genesis fit in with evolution?

Genesis is not meant to fit in with evolution. The author had no knowledge of evolution and, thus, no intention of giving an era-by-era account of how the world evolved. For instance, the six days of creation are just six ordinary days which he uses to organize his material. They have nothing to do with evolutionary periods.

56. Even so, aren't the Bible and evolution in contradiction?

It all depends on what kind of evolution. The Bible certainly contradicts any evolutionary theory which does not allow for real "jumps" or newness in the evolutionary chain. But modern evolutionary theory is quite open to real "jumps." Thus, modern evolutionary theory is not in contradiction to Genesis' teaching on the very real difference between man and animals.

The real problem with evolutionary theory is a scientific one of *verification*. When we look backward, we have what surely look like links in an evolutionary chain. But, when we work forward, we do not seem to be able to *predict* what will come next in evolution. Yet, accurate prediction is absolutely necessary if any scientific theory is to be verified.

MORAL LESSONS OF GENESIS

57. What is contained in the rest of the first eleven chapters of Genesis?

After the creation-accounts, the author rapidly sketches the origins of human society down to the time of Abraham, about 1850 B.C. What he does is to take certain features of Mesopotamian society as he knew it and use them to *illustrate* how certain features of society came into being. Interspersed with this are some rather fanciful genealogies, origin unknown, which list the peoples, lands, and inventions with which his readers were familiar.

58. Can you give some examples of how the author of Genesis illustrates the origin of the society he was familiar with?

a) The conflict between settled farmer and nomadic herdsman is traced back to the very beginning of time in the story of Cain and Abel. This story illustrates how violence entered the world.

b) The disastrous floods of the Mesopotamian plain are accounted for by the story of Noah and the ark. This story illustrates how helpless man is in the face of nature's enmity.

c) The contruction of a great Babylonian ziggurat (steppyramid) occasions the story of the Tower of Babel. This story illustrates man's total confusion in seeking after gods of his own making.

59. Do you mean that there actually weren't a Cain and Abel, a flood, and a Tower of Babel?

As far as the religious message of Genesis is concerned, the literal reality of these stories is irrelevant. The author is writing a moral tale, not history. And the moral of the story is rather pessimistic: Man and society are in an unholy mess.

60. Does the author of Genesis suggest any motive for God's creation?

Not directly. But he does describe creation as *good*, over and over. God takes delight in creatures just being themselves. The suggestion is irresistible: God's delight in his own existence is what impels him to create. The notion that it's *fun* to be alive is unique to Judaism and its daughter-religions.

61. For what sort of religion do the opening chapters of Genesis prepare us?

A salvation-religion. That is, a religion in which God takes the initiative in reestablishing familiar relations with man. All religions are concerned about the relation between God and man. Some religions do not believe that this relation can or need be improved. But salvation-religions believe that God has a transformation of his relation to humankind in mind—and intends to do something about it.

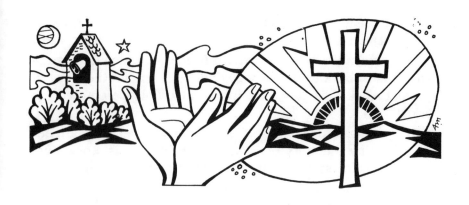

Chapter 3

THE STORY OF SALVATION

KINDS OF BOOKS IN THE OLD TESTAMENT

62. Is the rest of the Old Testament as hard to interpret as the opening chapters of Genesis?

No, it is not. Of course, the Old Testament is a collection of books, not a single book. So, knowing what type of literature each book is does help in understanding it.

63. What main types of books are contained in the Old Testament?

The first five books of the Bible (Genesis through Deuteronomy) occupy a unique place. They are the *Torah* or "law." The rest of the books are classified as "prophets" if they have to do with the very formation of the Jewish religion or "writings" if they apply or exemplify Jewish thought.

However, "prophets" and "writings" are rather strange classifications to a non-Jewish mind. So, another classification has also been found convenient: (a) *historical* books which narrate the main events of Jewish history; (b) *prophetic* books which explore and interpret Jewish religion; (c) *wisdom* books which teach by way of proverb or story how Jewish life is to be lived.

64. Is the "Torah" or "law" a code of laws as we understand it?

Not exactly. The *Torah* does contain codes of laws, especially the Ten Commandments (Ex 20:2-17 and Dt 5:6-18). But, more to the point, Genesis through Deuteronomy records the founding events, the personalities, and the attitudes which shape all of Jewish life. The *Torah* is a way of life; all else in the Old Testament is a commentary on it.

65. What do you mean by "prophecy" or a "prophetic book"?

"Prophecy" in the Bible means simply a religious message recognized as authentic by the believing community. A prophet is one who speaks for God. In the narrow sense, a prophetic book is one which records the words of an inspired *preacher*. The Old Testament prophets have aptly been described as "the conscience of Israel."

66. Aren't prophetic books predictions or visions of the future?

Only occasionally and only incidentally do the prophetic books describe the future. The biblical prophet is a preacher, not a seer. In order to form the consciences of his hearers, he may project the consequences of their actions into the future. Or, in order to console and encourage his hearers, he may project an idealized future which will occur when their present sinfulness is atoned for.

67. But there are visions in the Bible, aren't there?

There is a type of prophetic book called *apocalyptic* or revelatory. Ezekiel and Daniel in the Old Testament and the Book of Revelation in the New Testament are such books. An apocalyptic writer has his *imagination* directly affected by divine inspiration and, thus, he speaks and writes in symbols and imagery. But the symbols and imagery are concerned with the time and concerns of his readers. They are not detailed and literal descriptions of the future.

DIVINE INSPIRATION

68. Why does the Old Testament contain such a mixture of books?

The only real answer is because God inspired different sorts of authors to write different sorts of books. Both Old and New Testaments are a record of a community's grapplings with a self-revealing of God. The record contains just about every sort of literature as a means of expressing this overwhelming fact.

69.   But if all the books of the Bible are inspired by God, why is there no uniformity of style or approach in them?

Because divine inspiration is not dictation by God. Divine inspiration affects the *author's* talents, enabling him to produce a work containing nothing but God's message.

70.   Does this mean that the books of the Bible are not literally true?

All the books of the Bible are authentic statements of one religious message. But not all are the same sort of literature. The exuberant poetry of a prophet is not the same as the dry sentences of a chronicler. The satire and exaggeration of the book of Jonah (the Bible's "tall story") is not the same as the sober statements of a scribe.

The true-to-life story of David in the first book of Samuel (ch. 16ff) is not the same as the portrait of the legendary king in the first book of Chronicles (ch. 11ff). Asking why the author of Chronicles was inspired to idealize David is like asking why every culture needs its King Arthur and its Camelot.

71.   Can a divinely inspired book contain any errors?

A divinely inspired book cannot *misinform* its readers, provided one understands the human limitations of its author. There are slips in style and grammar, ordinary cases of mistaken identity or misunderstood sources in the Bible. Nor should we expect divine inspiration necessarily to broaden the author's outlook or to reveal to him something which he simply did not know. For instance, the author of the book of Job writes his inspired drama of the problem of evil without ever being aware that the imbalance between good and evil might be redressed in an afterlife.

VERSIONS OF THE BIBLE

72. How is it that the books of the Bible are known to be divinely inspired?

The *community* to which these books were addressed recognized their divine inspiration. It was the community, and not necessarily the author, which recognized that only these books expressed its precise understanding of God. In the case of the whole Bible, it was the Church which recognized and declared its divine inspiration.

73. How accurately have the books of the Bible been preserved?

Very accurately. As we discover more ancient texts, only minor corrections have to be made. Some sentences have been transposed, a few verses have become unintelligible (e.g., Ps 141:6-7), and some verses, notably the original ending of Mark's gospel, are lost. But that is all.

74. Why are some Old Testament books not contained in the Protestant Bible?

The Protestant translators followed the Palestinian list of books. This list included only Old Testament books written in Hebrew. Catholic Bibles include the non-Hebrew "apocrypha" as equally inspired because they contain the same message as the Hebrew books. Why the Hebrew language should be the criterion for divine inspiration is a bit puzzling.

75. Is there any difference between Protestant and Catholic translations of the Bible?

Any Bible published since the 1940s contains the best of both Protestant and Catholic research. But the *format* of a Protestant Bible is different. Protestants, generally, believe in letting God's word speak for itself. Thus, Protestant Bibles will contain notes only when there are textual variations or alternative translations. Catholics believe that the experience and tradition of the Church in reading the Bible should be available to the reader. Thus, footnotes in Catholic Bibles will contain explanatory and interpretative material as well.

THE PATRIARCHS

76. So—may we begin the story of salvation in the Old Testament?

Indeed, we should. It begins with the story of the patriarchs: Abraham, Isaac, and Jacob. (Genesis, chapters 12—36.)

77. What is the religious message of the story of the patriarchs?

Certainly, there is the germ of monotheism, i.e., the notion that there is one *only* God. But more to the point, there is the message that the one God has entered into human history and expects men to respond responsibly to his actions.

The one God calls the patriarchs to break with pagan culture and pagan gods. In return, the one God promises to make their descendants into a "mighty nation," i.e., a force rivaling the pagan empires among which they would wander. All this is diametrically opposed to ancient paganism. Not even the gods can do anything to change the everlasting order of the world and human life.

MOSES

78. What comes after the story of the patriarchs?

The migration of Jacob and his twelve sons to Egypt, the enslavement of their descendants, their wondrous deliverance from Egypt, the covenant and law at Mount Sinai, their wandering in the desert, and their entrance into Canaan. Moses is the great figure in this part of the Bible.

The main line of the story begins with chapter thirty-seven of Genesis, runs through the book of Exodus, and concludes with the book of Numbers. Included in the story are two great legal codes: the practical and detailed book of Leviticus and the poetic and mystic discourses of Moses composed by the author of the book of Deuteronomy.

79. What is the religious message of the story of Moses?

The story of Moses records *the* saving action of God around which all Jewish history revolves. That great event is the exodus from Egypt, around 1250 B.C. God's will overcomes the forces of nature and the power of a god-king in order to deliver his people. God's covenant and law enable his people to order their lives as free and responsible individuals. Paganism never saw religion as *liberating* mankind; Judaism and its daughter-religions do.

80. What is the supreme revelation made to Moses?

In the third chapter of Exodus, God reveals his sacred name: YHWH. It is pronounced "Yahweh" as near as we can determine. "Yahweh" is a mysterious form of the Hebrew verb "to be" or "to live." Since it is not a noun, The Name forbids the representation of God under any familiar form. As a verb-form, The Name indicates God's intention to be a living and acting presence among men. "Yahweh" is usually translated He-Who-Is.

God speaks to Moses out of the burning bush (see Ex. 3:2ff).

JUDGES AND EARLY KINGS

81. What happens after the time of Moses?

Under men and women of religious genius called "judges," the Israelites conquer and settle parts of Canaan. They demand a king and Samuel, greatest of the judges, anoints Saul. Saul fails and is replaced by the great warrior-king, David (about 1000 B.C.). Jerusalem is captured and Solomon, who succeeds his father, builds the temple of Yahweh.

Under Solomon, a Jewish empire comes into being. Prophets begin to appear who reproach king and people with failure to live by the spirit of God's covenant and law. The main line of the story runs through the books of Joshua, Judges, the two books of Samuel, and the first book of Kings, chapters 1—11.

A charming story, the book of Ruth, pictures life during the period of the judges. An idealized version of the lives of David and Solomon, written several centuries later, is found in the first book of Chronicles and the second book of Chronicles, chapters 1—9.

82. What is the religious message in the story of the judges and early kings?

It is the message that religion consists in true inner faithfulness. Neither power nor wealth excuses a person from humble and faithful obedience to God's law. Gradually, the notion that religion involves a good *conscience* is evolving. Yahweh is not content with mere ritual observances as the pagan gods are.

THE EXILE

83. What happens after Solomon?

In 931 B.C., the kingdom splits in two: Israel in the north and Judah in the south. Prophetic activity intensifies in each kingdom as kings and people accommodate Yahweh more and more with pagan divinities. (The main line of the story is told from chapter twelve of the first book of Kings through the whole of the second book of Kings. Another more idealized version of the same story is told in chapters ten through thirty-six of the second book of Chronicles.)

Now the Jewish people are caught up in the power-struggles of the great middle-eastern empires. In each kingdom, prophets warn of destruction: Amos and Hosea in the north; Micah, Zephaniah, Nahum, and Habakkuk in the south. Above all, the two great prophets Isaiah (8th cent. B.C.) and Jeremiah (7th cent. B.C.) deliver their inspired messages to the kings and people of Judah. Heedless of these preachers, kings and people continue on their way to destruction.

In 721 B.C., the Assyrians destroy the northern kingdom completely and its inhabitants are lost to history. The tiny kingdom of Judah holds out until 587 B.C., when the Babylonians capture Jerusalem, destroy the temple, and send the principal families into exile. During the exile, prophecy continues but gets more apocalyptic, reflecting the anguished and uncertain times (Ezekiel and Daniel).

84.   What is the religious message of the downfall and exile?

The core of the message is the *spirituality* of true religion. Religion is carried by the spirit of the individual and the community, no matter where they may be. Yahweh can do without the externals of land and temple; his land and temple are the hearts of those who worship him.

85.   What two great features of Judaism evolve during the exile?

During the exile, the great prophets develop fully the implications of *monotheism:* Yahweh's worship is the only true and meaningful worship there is; he is the God of all men and all nations. Likewise, during the exile, the idea of a *Messiah* (Anointed One) received its fullest development. The Messiah is the incarnation of the values of a purified Judaism. As such, the Messiah wins forgiveness for a sorrowing people.

Sometimes, the Messiah is pictured as a reincarnation of Moses; sometimes, he is thought of as a reincarnation of David. Most mysteriously, the Messiah is conceived of as a humble and suffering slave bearing the blame of all the people. (The servant-Messiah is found in Isaiah, chapters 40—55, a section written probably by disciples of Isaiah in continuance of his prophetic mission.)

THE RETURN

86.   Does the exile come to an end?

Yes, it does. In 538 B.C., Cyrus the Great, emperor of Persia, allows the deported Jews to return home. Under the leadership of Ezra and Nehemiah, a remnant return—their books tell the story. Jerusalem and the temple are painfully rebuilt and some semblance of national life is restored.

The Israelites begin to rebuild the Temple (see Ezr 1—6).

Prophecy slowly comes to an end with inspired messages of encouragement (Haggai, Zechariah, Malachi, Joel, and, perhaps, Obadiah). The Jewish community begins to record its hard-won experience in the Wisdom Literature of the Bible. (Much of this literature is hard to date but possibly Job, Proverbs, many psalms, the Song of Songs, Jonah, and Tobit belong to this period.)

87.   What is the religious message of the post-exilic period?

The core of the message is the importance of the *community,* its tradition and its attitudes, as the place where religion develops. Religion involves responsiveness to a tradition in Judaism and its daughter-religions. During the post-exilic period, the *synagogue,* a community school, almost overshadows the temple in religious importance.

88.   Are the Jews left in peace after the exile?

No, they are not. World forces overwhelm them again when Alexander the Great, almost casually, conquers Palestine on his way to Egypt (333 B.C.). Under Greek domination, the Jewish community continues to record its experience in books such as Ecclesiastes, Esther, and Sirach. Finally, the community is put under pressure and, then, persecuted to force its cultural assimilation.

Under the Maccabees (166-63 B.C.), the people temporarily regain their independence—the story is told in two books. The little book of Judith probably belongs to this period also. Independence does not last, however. In 63 B.C., the Romans capture Jerusalem and govern the land by a series of puppet-kings. About 50 B.C., the book of Wisdom is written and the Old Testament record is complete.

ISRAEL AT THE TIME OF JESUS

89. Who are the rulers of Palestine during the time of Christ?

At the time of Christ's birth, the most famous Roman puppet-king is the ruler of all Palestine, Herod the Great (37-4 B.C.). After his death, three of his assorted sons split the kingdom with Roman approval. In 6 A.D., Archelaus is deposed as ruler of Judea and the Romans appoint procurators to rule this section of Palestine directly. When Christ begins to preach, Herod Antipas is ruler in Galilee (4 B.C.-39 A.D.) and Pontius Pilate is procurator of Judea (26-36 A.D.).

90. What was the religious state of Judaism when Christ began to preach?

"It was the best of times, it was the worst of times." Jewish institutions held firm and the ordinary people held firm to them. Jewish leaders did not know whether to accommodate a bit to the Romans (Sadducee party) or to have nothing at all to do with them (Pharisee party). Scribes, learned in the law, mostly of the Pharisee party, were looked up to and respected by the community as its natural religious leaders. Some devout Jews had withdrawn totally from society into inaccessible communes (Essenes). More and more, Judaism prepared itself for another purification by Yahweh and waited for his word to come.

THE WORD BECAME FLESH AND MADE HIS DWELLING AMONG US (Jn 1:14).

Chapter 4

THE LIFE OF JESUS

THE NEW TESTAMENT

91. Where do Christians get their basic understanding of Jesus Christ?

The whole of the New Testament contains Christianity's basic understanding of Jesus. As the New Testament is printed today, it consists of:

a) The four gospels: Matthew, Mark, Luke, and John.

b) The Acts of the Apostles—a history of the founding of the Church.

c) Nine letters of St. Paul addressed to various Christian communities: Romans, 1 and 2 Corinthians, Galatians, Ephesians, Philippians, Colossians, 1 and 2 Thessalonians.

d) Three letters attributed to Paul addressed to Christian pastors: 1 and 2 Timothy, Titus.

e) One brief personal letter of Paul: Philemon.

f) A letter by an unknown author to Jewish Christians: Hebrews.

g) Seven letters of various apostolic origin addressed to all Christians: James, 1 and 2 Peter, 1, 2 and 3 John, Jude.

h) One apocalyptic book: Revelation.

92. How does each book of the New Testament contribute to an understanding of Jesus?

The New Testament, like the Old Testament, is an inspired record of a community grappling with God's self-revelation. One may read any book at random to discern the significance of Jesus in that self-revelation and the consequences of that significance in the lives of those who believe in Jesus. For instance:

a) One may read Galatians and then Romans (written in 57-58 A.D.) to discover how Christians defined their identity. versus Judaism because of the salvation won by Jesus Christ.

b) One may investigate the significance of Jesus in the two formal instructions on Christ which begin the letters to the Colossians and the Ephesians (written 61-63 A.D.).

c) One may read the sustained meditation on Christian salvation in the first letter of John.

d) One may read of the shared life between Jesus and the believer eloquently presented in the first letter of Peter.

e) One may read of the problems of the infant Christian communities in the two letters to the Thessalonians (written 50-51 A.D.) and the two letters to the Corinthians (written 57 A.D.).

93. Are any books of the New Testament absolutely central to understanding Jesus?

Yes, the four gospels are the central books of the New Testament. Even though they were not the first books of the New Testament to be written, the gospels present the sort of instruction about Jesus which the earliest Christians received orally. Thus, it is appropriate and traditional to present Jesus by means of the gospels and to use the other books of the New Testament to enrich and interpret the significance of the gospels. That is how Christians, down through the ages, learned their faith.

HOW THE GOSPELS WERE FORMED

94. Are the four gospels biographies of Jesus?

No, they are not. All of them present their material very much according to the way the apostles *preached*. It must be remembered that a whole generation of Christians heard the story of Jesus before the first gospel was written. As the New Testament stands today, this was Mark's gospel written about 64 A.D.

95. Does this mean that the evangelists (gospel-writers) did nothing but reproduce apostolic preaching?

The evangelists were certainly limited by a set way of telling about Jesus. This is especially true of the first three gospels: Matthew, Mark, and Luke. They follow a quite similar pattern. For this reason, they are called the "synoptic" gospels because they can be read side-by-side. John's gospel is independent of the pattern which indicates that it was written much later when the story could be told less rigidly.

96. How does this dependence upon apostolic preaching determine the arrangement of the synoptic gospels?

The synoptics have to lump together much material describing events which took place at different times and places in Jesus' life. For example, Mark puts all of Jesus' parables on one single day. However, they will add to or clarify each other. And, when the pattern does not limit them, they will introduce diverse material such as in Matthew's and Luke's varying accounts of Jesus' conception and birth.

97. How does apostolic preaching present the life of Jesus?

St. Peter's instruction to the pagan centurion, Cornelius (Acts 10:34-43), exemplifies the basic points of primitive instruction:

a) Jesus appears in Galilee preaching and healing.

b) He journeys to Jerusalem with his disciples.

c) In Jerusalem, he is crucified by connivance of some Jewish leaders.

d) On the third day, he rises from the dead, appears to his disciples, commissions them to proclaim the gospel, and is taken from their sight to the right hand of God.

98. Does each of the four gospels have a distinctive theme?

Yes, each evangelist has his own way of presenting Jesus. Matthew arranges the deeds and discourses of Jesus as stages in the coming of the kingdom of heaven. Mark contrasts the humility and suffering of Jesus with his final manifestation as God's chosen one. Luke follows Mark's theme but presents Jesus as the one who journeys to Jerusalem to inaugurate a new covenant. John pays more attention to the actual times and places when Jesus said or did something. John sees every detail of Jesus' words and actions as revealing God's saving presence in the world.

THE BIRTH OF JESUS

99. Do all the gospels tell of Jesus' birth?

No, only Matthew and Luke tell the familiar Christmas story. One verse in John speaks of the mysteriousness of Jesus' origin (Jn 1:13).

"The virgin shall be with child and give birth to a son . . ."
(Mt 1:23)

100. What is the doctrine of Jesus' virgin birth?

This doctrine derives from the evangelists' emphasis on the unlikeness of Jesus' human origin to ours. It is the doctrine that Jesus' human origin is a work of God's Holy Spirit in the womb of Mary. Jesus' conception, being a work of the Holy Spirit, is untouched by man's original sin. Nothing sinful can be produced by the Spirit of God.

101. What is the doctrine of the perpetual virginity of Mary?

It is the doctrine that Jesus was Mary's sole-begotten son. The evangelists, especially Luke, imply that Mary's whole person and life were absorbed in God's saving plan. That plan, incarnate, was her son. She not only gave him human life; she gave her life to his mission. This doctrine explains the Catholic reverence for Mary, Mother of Jesus and holiest of God's saints. We shall explore it more deeply in a later lesson.

102. Who are the brothers and sisters of Jesus mentioned in the gospels?

They are close relatives either by blood or by law. Villagers in Palestine, like villagers everywhere, made no careful distinction between degrees and sorts of relationship. All were "family."

DOCTRINE OF THE INCARNATION

103. Is the doctrine of Jesus' virgin birth the same as the doctrine of the Incarnation?

No, the doctrine of the Incarnation is the full statement of exactly *who* Jesus is. Jesus is the eternal Son of the heavenly Father born in the flesh from Mary. The doctrine of the Incarnation cannot be derived from just the accounts of Jesus' birth, wondrous as that birth was. The doctrine is derived from the whole of the gospels as their details reveal the identity of Jesus.

104. Even if Jesus' identity is not fully explicit in the narratives of his birth, could you state the full doctrine of the Incarnation?

Three centuries of thought were needed to get the precise words to state the doctrine of the Incarnation. It is this: Jesus is *one person* existing fully in *two natures,* divine and human. If you ask *who* Jesus is, he is no other than the eternal Son of God. If you ask *what* Jesus is, he is both fully divine and fully human.

105. What is the point about Jesus' "person" and "natures"?

This technical language was devised to prevent error in thinking and talking about Jesus. If Jesus were someone else than the eternal Son of God, then his claim to know God personally would be sheer blasphemy. On the other hand, if the eternal Son of God did not personally take on our humanity, then the claim that Jesus saved humankind by his human deeds would simply be untrue. (See Gal 4:4-7 for a New Testament statement of what, eventually, became the technical doctrine of the Incarnation.)

106. Are there any practical consequences in Christian life which follow from the doctrine of the Incarnation?

Yes, there are. Since Jesus' humanity is truly the personal humanity of the Son of God, one in divinity with the Father, then it follows that she who bore him according to the flesh is truly the mother of God. That Mary is truly the mother of God is Catholic doctrine, solemnly proclaimed at the Council of Ephesus in 431 A.D. It also follows that the hands of Mary's son which blessed and healed are truly the hands of God; the blood he shed on the cross is truly the blood of the eternal Son of the heavenly Father. This explains the deep Catholic devotion to various aspects of Jesus' humanity, such as his sacred heart or precious blood.

107. Can a knowledge of the full doctrine of the Incarnation lead to a misunderstanding of what the gospels tell us about Jesus?

Unfortunately, it can. We can assume it is the divine nature of Jesus which explains everything wondrous in the gospels, such as Jesus' miracles, his reading of hearts, his foreknowledge, etc. This, however, is not the way the gospels picture Jesus. They were not written primarily to prove Jesus' divinity. (See Phil 2:5-11 for a New Testament statement about Christ's earthly existence.)

WHAT THE GOSPELS PROVE

108. If the gospels are not primarily intended to prove Jesus' divinity, what are they trying to prove?

The gospels are trying to show how the Son of God, *as man,* became Lord of creation (the synoptics) or manifested himself as Lord (John). It is Jesus' human life of total obedience to the heavenly Father which wins for him, as man, everlasting life and the power to save all humankind from sin.

109. Don't the gospels present Jesus as divine at all?

The gospels show that Jesus, even as a child (Lk 2:41-50), was conscious of who he was and why he was sent by the Father. Beyond that, the evangelists refrain from picturing

Jesus' inner state of mind. But, as far as his extraordinary powers go, the gospels rather clearly ascribe them to his humanity as gifted by the Holy Spirit. (See Lk 4:16-22 for an explicit statement.)

110.   Aren't the extraordinary powers of Jesus rooted in his divine nature?

The gospels do not picture them that way. The extraordinary powers of Jesus are the gifts of the Holy Spirit to the Messiah. For instance, Jesus' miracles are never pictured as divine prodigies. Rather, they are signs that the Messianic age is dawning. (See Jn 2:11, 3:2, 6:29-30, 7:31, 9:1-39 for one evangelist's consciousness of the significance of Jesus' miracles.)

111.   But doesn't Christianity hinge on proving that Jesus was divine?

Not exactly. Christianity hinges on proving that Jesus was the Son of God born in our flesh to save us from sin. The gospels show how Jesus became (or was manifested) Lord at his resurrection. One then reads back and wonders just *who* could have managed such a task. The largest consideration is the *authority* with which Jesus speaks and acts. If it is anything less than the authority of One who fully communicates in the divinity of the heavenly Father, then the claims that Jesus makes are sheer blasphemy. Even Jesus' enemies recognized this (see Lk 22:67-71).

JESUS' PREACHING ON THE KINGDOM OF GOD

112.   On what do the gospels (especially the synoptics) spend most time in showing us of Jesus?

Following the pattern of apostolic preaching, they first tell of Jesus' appearance and activity in Galilee (northern Palestine). He emerges from the village life of Nazareth and, to indicate the new direction of his life, accepts ritual purification from his cousin, John. After a period of fasting and prayer, he begins to preach the imminent arrival of the kingdom of God and works the wonders of compassion and healing described in the Messianic prophecies.

He chooses disciples to observe and learn from him. Gradually, he comes into conflict with a segment of the Jewish authorities. They resent the authority with which he preaches and they fear the popular enthusiasm he is stirring up. More and more, Jesus devotes his time to the instruction of his disciples and withdraws from public view. Finally, he journeys to Jerusalem with them, predicting his own suffering, death, and resurrection, and the final judgment of the world.

113. How did Jesus teach the imminent arrival of the kingdom of God?

Jesus taught about the kingdom mostly in parables. A parable (Hebrew *mashal*) is a puzzle, provoking the hearer to thought. Parables were commonly used by all Jewish rabbis. Most of Jesus' parables are simple stories or comparisons; some are full allegories in which every detail has a meaning. The greatest collection of Jesus' parables is found in Luke, chapters 8—18.

Jesus teaches the people in parables (see Lk 8:1ff).

114. How can one best interpret the parables of Jesus?

It is not wise to find significance in every detail of a parable. Usually, Jesus' parables are just simple comparisons. For instance, the parable of the wily manager (Lk 16:1-8) is a comparison between the forethought of a worldly-wise man and the forethought a true disciple should have. In no way is the embezzlement of the manager being commended by Jesus.

115.   What does the expression "kingdom of heaven" or "reign of God" mean?

The expression is not unique to Jesus. It comes from the prophets. It means the decisive action of God, the exercise of divine power by which the faith and life of Israel would stand vindicated before the pagan world.

Popular imagination, influenced by the more apocalyptic prophets, took the kingdom of God as involving the destruction of the Roman Empire and the restoration of the golden age of the Davidic monarchy. Even Jesus' disciples were not immune from this popular picture (see Acts 1:6-8 for a description of the disciples' state of mind even after Jesus' resurrection).

116.   What does Jesus teach about the kingdom of heaven?

It is hard to give a coherent interpretation of Jesus' parables on the kingdom because they were probably responses to specific questions. But one can list some themes which run through the parables.

a) The kingdom requires conversion of life from sin to discipleship.

b) The dispossessed of the earth are especially ready to seek out the kingdom.

c) Discipleship demands detachment from worldly goods, humility, service, and faithful observance of the spirit of God's laws.

d) Entrance into the kingdom gives one serenity of spirit.

e) The kingdom is something inward and hidden, working a change in the whole person.

f) The kingdom will reach fulfillment at the judgment when what is unworthy in it will be purified.

117.   What is the essence of the teaching on the kingdom?

Perhaps it is best stated in one of Jesus' shorter parables: "Every scribe who is learned in the reign of God is like the head of a household who can bring from his storeroom both the new and the old" (Mt 13:52). Jesus is preaching an inner transformation in every element of Judaism. He is proclaiming a transformation in the covenant, the law, and the community. The "scribe who is learned" will discover what the whole of Judaism was aimed at accomplishing.

118.   Does the preaching of Jesus state what the new covenant, the new law, and the new community are going to be?

No, it does not. Perhaps even Jesus originally thought that the kingdom would just happen as he preached. However, as his public ministry progresses, his preaching on the kingdom aims at making *disciples* who will both witness and share in the new covenant, law, and community as they come into being.

Jesus' teaching and example *show* the new relation to God which he came to proclaim. So, even today, one cannot just read the gospels as if they were a manual of Christian life. One must encounter them in preaching and personal meditation in order to acquire their spirit. Otherwise, the gospels are as much a dead letter as the Mosaic law was to the Pharisees.

JESUS' JOURNEY TO JERUSALEM

119.   If the kingdom of heaven is the theme of Jesus' activity in Galilee, what is the theme of the journey to Jerusalem?

It is the suffering, death, and resurrection of Jesus as well as the end of the world. This is the gospel-theme of the totally unexpected triumph of Jesus over his enemies and the inauguration of a new and final age of the world.

(The literary device of placing all of Jesus' teaching on judgment and the end of the world within the context of one single journey to Jerusalem is used by all the synoptics. It begins in Mt 16:21, Mk 10:32, and Lk 9:51. John does not use this literary device but, rather, records much of Jesus' teaching in connection with various journeys to Jerusalem on the occasion of the great Jewish feasts.)

120.   Who were Jesus' enemies?

Segments of the leadership of all the Jewish parties and sects seem to have resented and feared Jesus. The gospels, wisely, refuse to speculate about the virulence of their hatred. As the gospels see it, their enmity is demonic, an intensification of the sinfulness of humanity in the face of the graciousness of God.

121. Then we cannot blame the Jewish nation for crucifying Jesus?

Anti-Semitism is a sin. The gospels never assign the blame for Jesus' crucifixion to the whole nation. To this day, the Jews remain God's chosen people and, in his graciousness, he leads them by his law. For us Gentiles, the existence of the Jewish people is a reminder that *we* received grace absolutely undeservedly.

(For the deepest and most compassionate New Testament text on the role of Israel in Christianity, see Rom, chapters 9—11. Remember that its inspired author was Paul, himself once a devout Pharisee.)

122. Did Jesus foresee his own death and resurrection?

The gospels surely picture Jesus, quite solemnly, speaking of the details of his death and resurrection. How much of this the evangelists are reading back into the events we do not know. In any case, the gospels make the point that Jesus, consciously, lived in utter obedience and trust that his heavenly Father would not fail him nor let his work fail.

123. How literally should we take Jesus' discourse about the end of the world?

Probably not literally at all. He himself tells his disciples that he does not know when it will be; it is not part of his Messianic knowledge. Also, his descriptions of the end of the world are not original. They are borrowed from a stock set of apocalyptic images found in the Old Testament. (For instance, compare Mt 24:30 with Dn 7:13-14.)

What Jesus does teach is an *intensification* of both good and evil in the world, beginning with his own passion, death, and resurrection. This intensification will culminate in the final vindication of his disciples and the inauguration of the world-to-come.

Chapter 5

JESUS CHRIST, THE REDEEMER

JESUS' DEATH AND RESURRECTION

124. How do the gospels tell of Jesus' suffering and death?

The narrative of Jesus' passion and death must have been firmly set by apostolic preaching because all four gospels give a remarkably similar account:

a) Jesus eats a Passover meal with his disciples and then goes with them to a garden outside Jerusalem for prayer.

b) In the garden, Jesus is arrested by the temple guard led there by the betrayer, Judas.

c) Jesus is taken before the Jewish Sanhedrin (council) and condemned on a trumped-up charge of blasphemy while, outside, Peter denies him.

d) Jesus is then handed over to the Roman procurator, Pontius Pilate, and accused of proclaiming himself a king.

e) Pilate sees through the charge but, out of fear of a riot, condemns Jesus to death by crucifixion (the death reserved for a slave).

f) Jesus is scourged, crowned with thorns, and forced to carry the cross(beam) outside the city to a low hill called Golgotha.

g) At Golgotha, he is nailed to the cross and, after three hours, expires.

h) After ascertaining the fact of Jesus' rapid death, Pilate gives Joseph of Arimathea permission to entomb the body.

i) The entombment is hasty because it is the Sabbath-eve. Jesus is laid in a new rock tomb and a stone is rolled over the entrance to seal it. Some women disciples carefully note its location in order to return and complete the burial.

125. How do the gospels tell of Jesus' resurrection?

The four gospels give remarkably dissimilar accounts of Jesus' resurrection from the dead. (We shall take up the dissimilarities at the end of the lesson.) The kernel of the account is this: Around daybreak of the first day of the week, the women return to complete the burial. On arrival, they find the tomb standing open and empty. Celestial messenger(s) announce to them that Jesus has risen from the dead. Each evangelist then records various appearances of the risen Jesus to the disciples.

126. What is so special about the gospel account of Jesus' death and resurrection?

These gospel accounts, especially John's, show us Jesus establishing a new covenant, a new law, and a new community. Even more, they show them as being established on Jesus' own authority. He himself is the bond of the new covenant. The new law is the law of love. The new community is the Church.

A new ritual, the Lord's Supper, is given whereby the new community remembers Jesus and his teachings, especially on humble and loving service. Baptism is the new community's initiation-rite. Authority to preach and to forgive sin is entrusted by Jesus' promise of the abiding presence of the Holy Spirit.

REDEMPTION

127. By what right does Jesus establish a whole new covenant, law, and community?

Jesus' right to establish all this rests upon his accomplishment of humankind's redemption from sin. His passion, death, and resurrection establish a new relation of grace between God and man. Every page of the New Testament carries this message; it is the "Good News."

128. What does "redemption" mean?

Literally, it means "buying back." For instance, in ancient times a slave could often buy back his freedom. But the biblical notion is deeper. It connotes the idea of *vindication*. The one redeemed by God's saving action finds himself not only freed from sin but also finds his life justified and righteous in God's sight.

129. Is Jesus aware that his death will be redemptive?

Yes, he is. For instance, at the Last Supper, Jesus deliberately introduces a new ritual by which his disciples will remember him. "The Lord Jesus on the night in which he was betrayed took bread, and after he had given thanks, broke it, and said, 'This is my body, which is for you. Do this in remembrance of me.' In the same way, after the supper, he took the cup, saying, 'This cup is the new covenant in my blood. Do this, whenever you drink it, in remembrance of me' " (1 Cor 11:23-27, written 57 A.D.).

130. What redemptive significance does the Lord's Supper have?

The terms which Jesus used show his consciousness of the sacrificial nature of what he was about to do. His body is "given" and his blood "shed" (Lk 22:19-20). These are ritual Jewish terms describing a sacrifice. The Passover context of the meal cannot be overlooked.

Jesus is the lamb of a new Passover delivering a new Israel from God's wrath upon unbelievers. The ritual is Jesus' way of communicating what his death will accomplish. The Lord's Supper *proclaims* the significance of his death whenever it is celebrated (see 1 Cor 11:26-27).

THE REDEMPTIVE SACRIFICE OF JESUS

131. What is a sacrifice?

A sacrifice, as near as we can define it, is an act of *dedicating* something to the divinity. It can be dedicated by destroying it, but this is not necessary. Sometimes, a thing can be sacrificed by simply offering it to the divinity and then partaking of it in a sacred communion. A person can, in sacrifice, dedicate his whole life or certain actions to the service of the divinity.

132. What is a sacrifice meant to accomplish?

A sacrifice is meant to make the worshiper acceptable to the divinity. The notions of sacrifice and redemption are intimately linked. The worshiper and the divinity are in communion with each other.

133. In what did the sacrifice of Jesus consist?

The New Testament emphasizes the life-long *obedient love* of Jesus to the will of his heavenly Father. Because Jesus is both the eternal Son of God and the Messiah, he is both God's well-beloved and the representative of a repentant human race. Everything, then, that Jesus did had a universal significance and won God's gracious response to all humankind.

134. Doesn't the sacrifice of Jesus consist in his passion and death?

Here we run into a real problem. The New Testament never speaks of mankind's redemption without speaking of the death of Jesus. He was obedient unto death (Phil 2:8); he loved his disciples to the end (Jn 13:1). Yet all of Jesus' life was not mere prelude to the passion. The sense of Christian belief is that his incarnation began our redemption just as his resurrection completed it. In fact, many theologians have wondered whether Jesus would have had to die to accomplish our redemption if he had been received differently by those to whom he was sent.

135. What is so special about Jesus' passion and death?

There is no consistent doctrine on this point even though every Christian thinker realizes that there must be something special about the passion and death of Jesus. What might lie at the heart of the matter is this: Jesus' obedient love embraced even the ultimate mystery of human wickedness—the demonic urge we all have to destroy goodness if we cannot corrupt it. Yet, he did not turn aside from his task of reconciling mankind to God. That may well be precisely what accomplished our redemption.

THE MEANING OF THE RESURRECTION

136. What does the resurrection of Jesus have to do with his sacrificial death?

The two can never be thought of separately. The resurrection of Jesus is the Father's response to his obedient love, his seal of approval on Jesus' faithfulness. A Christian must never forget that *Jesus really died;* he "descended into hell" (i.e., the nether world). To all intents and purposes, his work was a failure and passed away with him.

Hence, the resurrection is not Jesus merely resuming his career after an unfortunate interlude. The dead Jesus is truly *restored* to life as first fruits of the new order of grace. Obedient love, even in the face of the mystery of evil, is shown to be the force which death can never conquer.

137. Isn't the resurrection what proves that Jesus is the Son of God?

True, the New Testament does put a proof-value on the resurrection of Jesus. Since death could not hold Jesus in its power, the resurrection shows that he was truly God's beloved and the promised Messiah (see Peter's first sermon in Acts 2: 14-36). But what the resurrection *proves* is not the primary theme of the New Testament.

138. What is the primary resurrection-theme of the New Testament?

It is the lordship of Jesus. Jesus is Lord of his own body; his disciples have trouble grasping the transformation wrought by the resurrection. Jesus is Lord of human history; he authorizes the apostles to act in his name, not in the name of Yahweh. The New Testament is clearly conscious that a new and final age in history has dawned.

The risen Jesus meets two of his disciples on the way to Emmaus (see Lk 24:13-35).

HOW THE GOSPELS TELL OF THE RESURRECTION

139. This makes it sound like the resurrection and lordship of Jesus became apparent all at once to the disciples. Don't the gospels spread the incidents of the resurrection over a period of forty days?

The forty-day period is not found in the gospels but in the Acts of the Apostles. The four gospels relate the incidents variously. In fact, it is impossible to get a coherent gospel-account of the resurrection except for the discovery of the open and empty tomb by the women disciples.

a) Matthew places the appearance and ascension of Jesus in Galilee on an undetermined day after the resurrection.

b) Mark implies the same as Matthew, though an ancient appendix to his gospel puts the whole resurrection-event on one day in Jerusalem.

c) Luke follows the same scheme as the appendix to Mark's gospel.

d) John relates the resurrection-events as occurring over a week in Jerusalem and then, in a conclusion, records another appearance in Galilee.

e) Paul in First Corinthians (15:1-8) records another list of appearances of the risen Jesus.

140. What are we to make of these confused accounts of the details of Jesus' resurrection?

The apparent confusion bears out what we said about the way the gospels were composed. Where the narrative was not set, each evangelist could introduce diverse material. In the resurrection-accounts, it looks very much as if each gospel-writer gave prime importance to an appearance of Jesus witnessed by a disciple (or disciples) known personally to the community for whom the gospel was written. That disciple's witness is direct confirmation of the resurrection for that community.

141. Even so, the details of the resurrection-accounts are strangely incoherent. Why don't the evangelists agree?

It is true that times and places in the resurrection-accounts are strangely blurred. This is partly because different witnesses are being invoked. But it is also because the resurrection and lordship of Jesus are one single thing for the evangelists. *Any* appearance of the risen Jesus is also a revelation of his lordship of heaven and earth. The actual sequence of appearances and actions is secondary. "Jesus is Lord" sums up the teaching of the gospels on the resurrection.

142. Yes, but doesn't the incoherence of the resurrection-accounts make it rather difficult to believe in Jesus' resurrection?

Frankly, too much coherence would make it more difficult to believe. One would strongly suspect that the evangelists (or their sources) cooked up the whole thing. The smoother the account of something totally unexpected and incredible, the more suspicious one becomes about what really happened. What underlies the great gospel-theme that Jesus *is* Lord are diverse witness-accounts of a genuine experience.

143. Granted that the disciples genuinely experienced something, couldn't it have been some sort of group-hallucination or group-illusion?

"Explaining" the resurrection of Jesus as some sort of abnormal state in the minds of the disciples has been tried over and over—sometimes for the best of reasons. But hallucination, especially for a whole group, simply won't fit the gospel-accounts.

Jesus appears to the disciples when they are in perfectly ordinary circumstances and in perfectly ordinary states of mind. Group-illusion will not work either, because Jesus is careful to clear up any possibility of misperception by inviting the disciples to examine him in familiar conditions.

144. What does the resurrection of Jesus have to do with my salvation?

"If Christ has not been raised, our preaching is void of content and your faith is empty too" (1 Cor 15:14). St. Paul does not mean just that it would be stupid to believe in Jesus if he lies buried somewhere outside Jerusalem. He means that the lordship of Jesus is a real force at work in the world. Because of it, our faith truly accomplishes something in *us*. Grace has taken its final and concrete form in the risen Jesus.

Chapter 6

JESUS CHRIST, THE LORD

SALVATION, UNION WITH JESUS

145. If the risen Christ is the very grace of God, then is it true that salvation is the same as union with Christ?

Yes, union with Christ is the same as salvation. Jesus says: "I am the vine, you are the branches. He who lives in Me and I in him, will produce abundantly, for apart from Me you can do nothing" (Jn 15:5).

146. Is this union with Christ the same as following the example and teachings of Jesus?

No, it is not. The example and teachings of Jesus are surely a Christian's life-pattern. But non-Christians have also admired and adopted the teachings of Jesus. Yet they have not believed in him as the eternal Son of God and redeemer of the human race.

147. What does a Christian find in the teachings of Jesus?

The path to eternal life. A Christian believes that Jesus invites his disciples to share in the personal communion he has with the heavenly Father in the Holy Spirit. For a Christian, to accept the redemption won by Jesus is to accept a whole new relation to God. It is this relation which is incomprehensible to a non-Christian.

148. Is union with Christ the same as accepting him as my personal savior?

Surely, the acceptance of salvation is a personal act which no one else can do for you. But it is not a strictly private affair. Those who would be disciples of Christ form a visible and identifiable *community*. In fact, their union in belief and life with each other is a sign of their union with Christ. (See Jn 17.)

149. Is belief in Christ as savior enough to make one a member of this community of disciples?

No, it is not. Faith in Jesus is surely the essential component of Christian discipleship. But *baptism* is the visbile ritual which initiates one into the community.

150. Does this mean that one must belong to the Church in order to be united with Christ?

Yes, it does. Union with Christ is accomplished by quite visible and identifiable means. All Christian communities believe that baptism is more than a mere ritual. It is truly a rebirth into eternal life. The earliest Christians already understood baptism as a share in Jesus' victory. "Are you not aware that we who were baptized into Christ Jesus were baptized into his death? Through baptism into his death we were buried with him, so that, just as Christ was raised from the dead by the glory of the Father, we too might live a new life" (Rom 6:3-9, written in 57-58 A.D.).

THE CHURCH AND CHRIST

151. Does this mean that there is no other way of being a Christian except in the Church?

There is no other way. St. Paul, for instance, would not have been able to make sense of one who claimed to be a Christian but was not joined "in the body" to other believers. Such a person would not be joined "in the body" to the Lord.

152. What is this "body" to which a Christian belongs?

Although it is presently a bit out of fashion, St. Paul's comparison of the Church to Christ's very continuing body is truly remarkable. The comparison has two parts:

a) As far as each individual church member is concerned, St. Paul sees his salvation as accomplished by a real share in what Christ accomplished "in the body," i.e., in his humanity. Thus, Paul can argue that no Christian can join his body to anything unworthy of the Lord. (1 Cor 6:13-20 emphasizes this part of the comparison.)

b) As far as the community of believers is concerned, St. Paul sees it as gifted, like the Lord's humanity, to carry on his saving work. The gifts of the Holy Spirit are parceled out in the Church. Individuals are "members" of this continuing body of Christ and their union with the Lord depends upon each using his gift for the good of all. (1 Cor 12:12-30 contains one of Paul's strongest statements of this part of the comparison.)

153. Are there any other New Testament comparisons which express the genuine union between the Church and Christ?

The New Testament is very rich in comparisons emphasizing the genuine union of the believing community with its Lord. Christ is the vine; believers are the branches (Jn 15:5). Christ is the bridegroom; the Church is his bride (Eph 5:21ff). Christ is the new Adam; believers are the new human race (Rom 6: 12ff). Christ is the high priest of a new covenant; believers are the new people of God (the whole letter to the Hebrews).

THE CHURCH — THE ABIDING PRESENCE OF CHRIST IN THE WORLD

154. Isn't this a very ideal and spiritual sort of Church?

Not at all. As it was in St. Paul's time, the Church today is a quite visible and identifiable community containing some less-than-ideal institutions and rather non-spiritual persons. Speaking properly, the Church is a *mysterion*. That is, the Church is the embodiment and sign of the continuing presence of the Lord Jesus in the world.

155. What does the word "mysterion" mean?

The Greek word *mysterion* means something not apparent to the uninitiated. Thus, when one speaks of the "mystery" of the Church or refers to the "mystical" body of Christ, one means that there is more to the Church than what meets the eye.

156. **What more is there to the Church than what meets the eye?**

What the Church embodies and signifies to the world is a genuine, abiding presence of the risen Jesus. Believers truly partake in the victory of the Lord over sin and death. Their lives and his are in continuity. That is the *mysterion.*

157. **What indicates to the world that there is more to the Church than its visible organization?**

No settled Church doctrine exists on this point. The Church, wisely, has contented itself with the wealth of New Testament imagery in its self-description. However, three models or ideals seem always to be at work as the Church presents itself to the world:

a) The Church tries to be a *fellowship* or *communion* of quite diverse persons in one faith and style of life.

b) The Church tries to be the *herald* or *prophet* of God's love for a sinful world.

c) The Church tries to be the *servant* and *healer* of those whom the world writes off.

Members of the parish council serve the parish.

158. **Is a Christian supposed to be conscious of these models or ideals of the Church?**

Not necessarily. What a Christian is conscious of are the gospel-values of self-forgetfulness, forgiveness, and charity. The Christian knows that he and his Church stand accountable to God if these basic gospel-values are not present, and proclaimed, and practiced in human life. They are what make the *mysterion* apparent.

THE CHURCH AND HUMANITY

159.   Aren't these gospel-values also basic human values?

Indeed, they are. Without them, no human community can long endure. That is the reason why the Church, in addition to its proper mission of proclaiming the gospel, also address itself to human problems in all their complexity. This lies at the root of Church pronouncements on many social issues.

160.   Isn't the Church out of its field in pronouncing on social problems?

It would be if the gospel-values were purely spiritual or otherworldly. But a Christian cannot make a neat distinction between the material and the spiritual. The proper distinction is between "here" and "hereafter." The kingdom of God is not something utterly unworldly. On the contrary, it is coming into being from what, precisely, is "here." Thus, the Church *cannot* ignore what is "here"—it is the stuff of the kingdom of God.

161.   Is the Church, then, supposed to make the world into the kingdom of God?

The safest thing to say is that the world *is* going to become the kingdom of God. It is also safe to say that the Church has an indispensable role in bringing about the kingdom because it is the embodiment and sign of the risen Jesus. Many a Christian thinker has pondered exactly what that role may be and not arrived at a satisfactory answer.

The reason for this may be that the Church is still making up what has to be undergone in order that Christ's presence be complete in the world. Thus, like Jesus before the resurrection, it lives in hope without knowing precisely what form the outcome of that hope will take. (For a more daring expression of this idea, see St. Paul's outpouring in Col 1:24-29.)

162.   How have all these ideas about the "mysterion" entered into everyday Christian consciousness?

Very simply—as simply as the New Testament puts them. A Christian's salvation consists in a union with the risen Lord. His religion consists in following the teachings of Jesus in thankfulness for God's grace. That is the "style" of Christianity. The

Christian lives in loving obedience to the commandments of God as taught and exemplified by Jesus. He loves and heeds the Church as his indispensable means of salvation. He shows to the world the gospel-values of self-forgetfulness, forgiveness, and charity.

163. Is a Christian supposed to work for the salvation of the whole world?

Yes, he is. The gospel-values are precisely what turn him outward to others. Through him, the *mysterion* which is the Church becomes manifest to the world.

164. Does this mean that a Christian is supposed to convert everybody to Christianity?

Here the individual Christian encounters the same problem which faces the whole Church. He has been given a call-to-faith and he knows that the Church is his sole means of salvation. He also knows that salvation consists in entering the kingdom of God. In working for the salvation of the world, is he thereby working to convert everyone to Christianity? The question is so important that we shall devote our next lesson to it.

Chapter 7

THE CHURCH AND THE WORLD

THE CHURCH AND SALVATION

165. Is everyone offered an opportunity for salvation?

Absolutely yes. Somewhere, somehow in everyone's life the grace of God is offered. The Bible is clear about God's will to save all humankind. Because of this saving will, all persons stand accountable before God in their consciences (Rom 2:7-11).

166. Does this mean that everyone is offered an opportunity sometime in life to become a member of the Church?

Unfortunately, no. Christianity, like all salvation religions, is a message. If it is not communicated, there can be no call-to-faith (see Rom 10:14-17). The distressing fact that countless men and women have lived and died without ever hearing of the gospel both urges the Church on its missionary endeavor and offers convincing evidence that God does not call everyone to faith in Jesus.

167. Does hearing the gospel automatically amount to a call-to-faith?

It seems not. Overzealous missionary activity can confuse a call-to-faith with a call-to-grace as if grace and faith are synonymous. Fortunately, modern missionaries have learned the distinction. In fact, the missionary who makes no converts may be "gracing" non-Christians in a way hidden in God's providence.

In a personal way, the missionary experiences the problem of the relation of the Church to the kingdom of God. His task is to make the *mysterion* manifest; God's response is to move the hearts of people toward salvation in His own mysterious ways.

168. But if Church membership is the same as union with the risen Christ, how can one who does not belong to the Church be saved at all?

That is the heart of the problem for a Christian. He firmly believes that Christ is God's final self-revelation. He firmly believes that all grace comes through Christ. And he firmly believes that the only abiding presence of Christ in the world is the Church. Somehow, then, it is *through* the Church that salvation comes even to one who does not belong to the Church.

169. Could it be that persons who do not belong to the Church are saved by some sort of spiritual membership in it?

Saying that someone belongs to the Church "spiritually" is unfair on two counts: (a) it amounts to making good, conscientious people members of a community to which they know perfectly well that they do not belong; (b) it amounts to saying that the Church is not a visible and identifiable community when it really is.

170. How is the non-Church member's salvation connected with the Church?

Just about every shade of opinion exists among theologians. One promising line of thought connects the salvation of the non-Church member with the *prayer* of the Church. Always, the Church makes intercession for all classes and conditions of humankind, especially the most helpless. The risen Lord prays in and through his Church and it is certain that his prayer cannot but be heard by his gracious Father.

171. Is the non-Chuch member's grace a share in Christ's resurrection?

No one really seems to know. If it were a share in Christ's resurrection, he would seem to be a member of the Church. But if his relationship to God had nothing to do with Christ, then it would not seem to be grace at all. Perhaps it is a presence of

Christ, "the Word . . . which gives light to every man" (Jn 1:9), illuminating and enlivening his religious convictions so that they became a response to a heavenly Father whose name he does not know.

172.   But if anyone can be saved, why is it better to be a member of the Church?

A distinction has to be made in order to answer this question. In real life, one who is given the call-to-faith is not being given the option between the Church and some other means of salvation. The Church *is* his sole means of salvation and God alone, in His graciousness, knows what it is about this person which makes it imperative that he work out his salvation in the Church.

In the abstract, one can ask what is better about salvation-in-the-Church compared to salvation-outside-the-Church. The answer is that the good acts of the Church member help bring on the kingdom of God. The good acts of the non-Church member save only himself. (That a Christian lives, suffers, even dies to make something *new* come into being is stated in the densely-packed words of Romans 8:14-30. The first three chapters of Ephesians represent the most carefully thought-out version of this great theme of St. Paul.)

173.   What about the salvation of unbaptized infants?

Christian good sense demands that an unbaptized infant who dies surely does not deserve condemnation by God. About the only formal teaching of the Catholic Church consistently censures the opinion that unbaptized infants go to hell.

Medieval theologians taught that unbaptized infants are in a state called "Limbo" (the fringe), naturally happy, but not sharing in the inner life of the divinity. But even the existence of Limbo has never become Catholic doctrine. For instance, the present Catholic burial rite for unbaptized infants makes no mention of Limbo but simply commends the infant to God's mercy.

The feel of Catholic thought is that the prayer of the Church, conjoined with the parents' natural desire for what is best for their child, wins God's grace for an unbaptized infant.

174. **Could someone be an actual member of the Church without being baptized?**

Yes. Catechumens (persons under instruction) who die before baptism have always been recognized as actual Church members because of their desire for baptism. All the more is their actual membership recognized if the catechumen was martyred for the sake of the faith.

Such Church membership is accomplished by a personal act of Christ responding to the catechumen's faith. By extension, it may also be the case that children whom parents intend to have baptized but who die accidentally before baptism are actually incorporated into the Church by their parents' desire and intention.

THE CHURCH'S SOCIAL MISSION

175. **After preaching the gospel and baptizing those called to faith, is the Church's mission to the world finished?**

It is surely the Church's *proper* mission to preach the gospel and to baptize those called to faith (Mt 16:15-16). That is to say, no one else is accountable to God for this task. But both Christian thought and Christian practice belie the notion that once the gospel has been preached and baptism administered the Church can tend to its own affairs and view human needs without concern. (For some trenchant remarks on faith without good works, see the letter of James 2:14-26.)

176. **What lies at the heart of the Church's social mission?**

The whole thrust of the gospel-values of self-forgetfulness, forgiveness, and charity ground the Church's social mission. These are what put a Christian at the disposal of a needy world. The world is his neighbor and he spontaneously recognizes it just as the good Samaritan (Lk 10:29-37), without any instruction, recognized his neighbor.

177. **Does the Church's social mission consist exclusively in works of charity?**

Many Christians seem to have the idea that the social mission of the Church should properly be confined to works of charity. But, important and needful as this service to humanity

On October 4, 1965, Pope Paul VI spoke out against war and social injustices before the United Nations General Assembly.

is, the world's needs have become larger. Thus, Church authorities, even though criticized and misunderstood, have not hesitated to speak out on social and economic issues.

178. By what right do Church authorities speak out on social and economic issues?

Sometimes it is the right of outraged Christian conscience. The denunciations of the Old Testament prophets and of Jesus himself provide the justification for speaking out in this manner. More often, church authorities speak out because of their pastoral obligations. Shepherding and encouraging the people of the Church, they feel the obligation to speak to all men of good will about the values of the gospel.

Although it is true that the Church is not of this world, it truly is in this world. The Church cannot act as if the gospel values were utterly otherworldly. Universalized, these are also the values of a genuine humanity.

179. What is the purpose of Church pronouncements on social and economic issues?

None of them pretends to be a concrete and detailed plan for political action. The Church, as an institution, would be beyond its competence in pronouncing on such matters. Rather, such pronouncements are an attempt to sensitize the conscience of Church members and all people of good will to a range of social and economic wrongs. In addition, pastoral pronouncements attempt to show the relevance of gospel-values to the humanizing of the conditions which have produced social and economic injustice.

180. What obligation does the individual Christian have in the face of Church pronouncements on social and economic issues?

The hardest thing for the Christian-in-the-pew is to accept them for exactly what they are without being overwhelmed by fruitless guilt-feelings or despairing over implementing their proposals. The problem sometimes lies with the preacher who has not properly studied all the nuances of the pronouncement.

Concerned Christians have marched against social injustice and questionably just wars.

The fault sometimes lies with the hearer who hopes for more from the pronouncement than the Church's competence can provide.

Such documents are no less than an appeal to conscience. And conscience is no more and no less than good judgment exercised by an individual on the complexities of human life from where his accomplishments have placed him with his individual insights and gifts.

Chapter 8

THE DIVIDED CHURCHES

THE INQUIRY AFTER CHRIST'S TRUE CHURCH

181. Do Roman Catholics think that their Church is the only true Church?

At times, official Catholic statements came perilously close to making this claim. But Catholic practice has always recognized genuine elements of Christ's Church in other Christian communities. The most accurate statement of Catholic belief is that Christ's true Church "subsists" in the Roman Catholic Church. This is the word which the second Vatican Council chose in its Dogmatic Constitution on the Church, article 8.

In less technical language, this means that the Roman Catholic Church is the full embodiment of Christ's Church. It does not mean that there are no genuine elements at all of Christ's Church embodied in other Christian communities.

182. What is one to make of the divisions among Christian Churches?

Quite simply, they are a scandal and a stumbling block to one who seeks salvation by union with the risen Christ. Yet, the scandal exists and must be faced.

183. How does one discover which Church most fully realizes the characteristics of Christ's true Church?

The inquiry into Christ's true Church has taken two forms: (a) a study of the "marks" of the Church; and (b) interfaith dialogue.

184. What are the "marks" of the Church?

The ninth article of the Nicene Creed reads: "We believe in one holy catholic [worldwide] and apostolic Church." This is the most ancient statement in Church tradition (451) about an *orthodox* conception of Christ's Church. Thus, it provides a standard against which to compare various Churches.

185. Are the four marks separate descriptions of Christ's true Church or are they a fourfold description of it?

It seems best to think of "one holy catholic and apostolic" as a fourfold description of one reality. Each of the marks guards and preserves the others. Weaken one, and you weaken all. Christ's true Church must teach in *integrity* all that Christ taught. Likewise, it must provide its members with all the means to God's *grace* given to us by Christ. Its membership must be *open* to any and all who seek salvation. Finally, it must be faithful to the *tradition* which goes back, generation after generation, to the apostles.

186. Is the Roman Catholic Church truly "one holy catholic and apostolic"?

Yes, it is fully. But saying that it is does not prove that it is. This whole catechism is meant to show that it is the full embodiment of Christ's Church. But, if an inquirer is not convinced, his conscience must lead him elsewhere.

187. Are the marks a sort of yardstick against which Churches are to be measured?

The authors of the Nicene Creed meant them to be just that. And, even though they have provoked quarrels between Christian bodies, it remains the fact that thoughtful men and women have discerned doctrinal wholeness, proven sanctity, transcultural adaptability, and historic continuity to be the necessary attributes of Christ's Church.

One cannot imagine a church which officially discards a teaching of Christ, does not demand that a value of the gospel be lived, identifies itself with a nation or a culture, and has no concern for the example given by the earliest Christian communities. There is, of course, no such actual church. But one might profitably read some of the great conversion-stories to see why sincere men and women did leave the Church of their upbringing for another.

ECUMENICAL PRINCIPLES

188. But, if Christ's Church subsists in the Roman Catholic Church, does this mean that Catholics have nothing to learn from other Churches?

In theory this statement might be true. But, in fact, the divisions in Christianity have wounded the Catholic Church, too. Actual styles of Christian life and worship exist strongly in other Churches which exist only weakly in the Roman Catholic Church. For example, the evangelical zeal and piety of Lutheranism, the fellowship of the Baptist communion, the Methodist concern with spiritual values—all are living reproaches to what Catholics should be. Something real has gone out of the Catholic Church and it is the poorer for it.

189. Is it even true in theory that Catholics have nothing to learn from other Churches?

Actually, no. If one pursues the deepest implications of the actual existence of Christ's Church amidst divided Christianity, it must follow that, wherever genuine elements of Christ's Church exist, there also is the real presence and working of the *one* Holy Spirit. Any Church, including the Catholic Church, must be responsive to the workings of the Holy Spirit if it is to be faithful to Jesus. Thus, the Catholic Church may well have to seek instruction and guidance from another Church wherever and whenever it discerns the plain workings of the Spirit.

190. If the one Holy Spirit is present and working wherever elements of Christ's true Church are found, does it follow that these elements are also the same?

Yes and no. Perhaps baptism may provide the clearest example of the sameness and divergence which is the tragic inheritance of divided Christianity. In a very real sense, one is both baptized Roman Catholic (for instance) and also baptized into Christ's true Church. In intent and in fact, the one who is baptized Roman Catholic is in communion with that Church and not, say, with the Methodist communion.

Yet, at the same time, there is but "one Lord, one faith, one baptism" (Eph 4:5). Thus, whoever is baptized into one Christian communion stands in the same redeemed relation to the heavenly Father as one who is baptized into any other. That is why baptism should never be readministered when a validly baptized person passes from one Christian Church into another.

191. Does the problem, then, lie with the Christian communion into which one is baptized rather than with the baptism itself?

Exactly. If the Christian communion is imperfect or defective as an embodiment of the Church's unity, holiness, catholicity, and apostolicity, then the Holy Spirit's work is impeded. Words like "imperfect" or "defective" are not the clearest language in which to express the sense of "something missing." Yet, any Christian who has become uncomfortable with his own Church senses the reality they mean.

192. Could a Roman Catholic ever admit that there might be something imperfect or defective about his church?

This question brings out the awkwardness of the language used to describe "something missing" in a Christian communion. In the ordinary sense of the words, a Roman Catholic would have no trouble at all in admitting that Roman Catholicism has had its share of imperfections and deficiencies throughout history.

However, as the words are used in theological writing, they signify an imperfection or deficiency in the very *constitution* or structure of a Church, no matter what its actual history. That is the way the words are used in ecumenical dialogue. In that sense, a Roman Catholic could not admit that his Church is imperfectly or defectively constituted.

ECUMENICAL DIALOGUE

193. What is ecumenical or interfaith dialogue?

In ecumenical or interfaith dialogue the participants try to discern, under the guidance of the Holy Spirit, the constitutive elements of Christ's Church and the extent of their presence in their respective communions. Realizing that Christ's Church is one household (*oikumene* in Greek), they seek after what unites them rather than what divides them. Really, the dialogue should be called in*tra*faith rather than in*ter*faith, but language seems to have settled on the latter. Much good to all Churches has occurred because of the patient listening and honest speaking of the participants in such dialogues.

After Vatican II, ecumenical gatherings with people of other religious persuasions have become common in the Church.

194. Are Roman Catholics in ecumenical dialogue primarily to reunite other Churches to Catholicism?

No one can bring about the union of the Churches except the Holy Spirit. Thus, Roman Catholics are in ecumenical dialogue precisely on a level with the other participants. However, the notion that the "Church of the future" could, under the guidance of the Holy Spirit, have no recognizable continuity with the Roman Catholic Church is incredible to *all* participants in ecumenical dialogue, not just to Catholics. Although it is hard to express, there is something central about Roman Catholicism in the history of Christianity.

Roman Catholics involved in ecumenical dialogue are confident that the "Church of the future," if and as the Holy Spirit brings it about, will be "Catholic." Whether it will reproduce point-for-point the institutions, customs, and church order of present-day Catholicism is another matter.

195. What have been the principal topics of ecumenical dialogue thus far?

When one realizes that ecumenical dialogue has been in progress not much more than a decade, one is amazed at how soon historical rancor among Christian communions has been laid aside. What has emerged is a common concern about what makes for *unity* in Christ's Church.

Although no one can predict where ecumenical dialogue will lead, two topics central to Church unity have emerged: (a) the eucharist as inner sign and cause of unity; and (b) the "Petrine ministry" as exterior sign and cause of unity. Although headlines such as "Non-Catholics Accept Mass and Pope" are surely premature, "Mass" and "Pope" are no longer fighting words among the Churches.

196. What else has ecumenical dialogue accomplished?

It has succeeded in identifying and suggesting ways to ameliorate pastoral problems which can arise when Christians of different communions must recognize and respect each other's convictions. The evident example is an interdenominational marriage. Recommendations from such dialogues are being studied and, in some cases, have been acted upon by appropriate church authorities.

197. Will ecumenical dialogue by itself bring about unity among the Churches?

Obviously not. Only the Holy Spirit can accomplish that. Even from a purely human level, discussion must be complemented by concrete and highly specific action if the unity among Christians is to become a felt reality to the person-in-the-pew. Unfortunately, all the Churches, under the stress of modern secularity, have turned somewhat inward to preoccupation with their own affairs. This sad fact may forestall the workings of the Spirit.

Chapter 9

INTERCHURCH COOPERATION

THE ROMAN CATHOLIC RELATIONSHIP TO OTHER CHURCHES

198. Are some Churches closer in doctrine and practice to the Roman Catholic Church than others?

Yes. The closest are the Orthodox Churches. Originally the Greek-speaking Churches of the eastern Roman empire, they gradually broke with the Latin-speaking West and finally, in 1054, Michael Cerularius, patriarch-bishop of Constantinople, rejected the primacy of the Pope. This schism (break) is the reason why Latin-rite Catholics are numerically the greatest. Actually, there are eastern-rite Catholics who never broke with Rome and also eastern-rite Catholics, once Orthodox, who have reunited with Rome.

199. What are the current relations between the Catholic and Orthodox Churches?

The Catholic Church recognizes the complete validity of the Orthodox priesthood and sacraments. Orthodox and Catholic faithful, in cases of spiritual necessity, may be served by each other's priests. A marriage between a Catholic and an Orthodox believer may be celebrated validly in either's Church.

200. What about Anglican or Episcopal Churches?

Anglicanism began simply as a rejection of papal authority under Henry VIII. But, in 1559, when the Church of England became the established religion under Elizabeth I, men of extremely Protestant outlook wrote the Church's creed and ritual. Catholics look sympathetically at Anglicans who are trying to recover their "Catholic" heritage. On an official level, the hardest Roman Catholic decision was the denial that Anglican ordinations confer a valid priesthood (Leo XIII, 1896).

201. What about Protestant Churches?

Church-to-Church relations between Roman Catholics and Protestant bodies vary considerably, depending on what Protestant Church is involved. When, in 1517, Martin Luther protested against the sale of indulgences, he rightly protested against one of the many corruptions in sixteenth-century Catholicism. But, by 1521, Luther's thinking had led him completely out of the Catholic Church. Luther's doctrine that salvation was won, once and for all, by personal faith in Jesus, led him toward the conclusion that the Church had no divinely-commissioned intermediary role to play in man's salvation.

Although Luther hesitated to draw the most radical conclusions of his position, others were not slow to do so. Thus, in extreme Protestantism, the Church is merely a human institution existing to help the individual believer as his needs dictate. Obviously, then, relations between Catholics and Protestants vary, depending on each's understanding of what the Church is and does.

SPECIFIC PROBLEMS OF INTERCHURCH RELATIONS

202. Could a Catholic and non-Catholic clergyman interchange functions?

They are surely interchangeable in functions which each Church recognizes as proper to a clergyman. Each could lead the other's congregation in prayer and could also exchange pulpits. So, too, in such pastoral ministry as the visitation of the sick, each could pray with and comfort members of the other's congregation.

203.   **Could a Catholic and non-Catholic clergyman administer sacraments to each other's congregations?**

In general, the answer is negative. Sacramental administration involves a denominational commitment and denominational belief. For instance, one is baptized Catholic or baptized Methodist. Thus, it would be out of place for a clergyman of one Church routinely to administer sacraments to one who is not a member of his communion.

204.   **How is it that the non-Catholic party to an interdenominational wedding can get married in a Catholic church?**

Marriage is a sacrament administered by the bride and groom. The priest is merely the *witness* to the wedding. Orthodox Christians, however, believe that the priest administers the sacrament. Practically, then, it is best that any marriage in which an Orthodox Christian is involved take place in the Orthodox Church.

205.   **Does it follow, then, that a Catholic party to an interdenominational wedding could just as well get married in a non-Catholic church?**

Until recently, this was forbidden by Catholic canon law. Now, however, the law exempts Orthodox Churches. The law now also allows a marriage between a Catholic and a Protestant to take place in a Protestant church if the minister has special ties of family or friendship to the Protestant party. Special permission of the Catholic bishop is needed for this wedding to be recognized as valid in Catholic law. Eventually, Church-to-Church agreements may eliminate this need for the bishop's permission.

206.   **Can a Catholic be a godparent at a non-Catholic baptism and vice versa?**

No, he cannot. Baptism involves a denominational commitment by the parties involved. A godparent is taking some responsibility for seeing to it that the one being baptized is raised according to the belief and practice of that denomination. A non-communicant cannot make such a commitment. The most graceful solution is to ask the non-communicant to serve as a Christian witness to the baptism. A Christian witness gives honor to the *person* being baptized without being involved in an embarrassing denominational commitment.

207. Can a Catholic be a best man or maid of honor at a non-Catholic wedding and vice versa?

Yes, he can. The best man or maid of honor are witnesses to the wedding. Their presence honors the couple being married and involves no denominational commitment.

208. Can a Catholic worship in a non-Catholic church and vice versa?

Arbitrary church-hopping is improper for any Christian. He owes worship, support, and personal commitment to the life of his own denomination. But, for good and sufficient reason, such as family or social ties, occasional worship in another church is proper. On such occasions, Catholic or non-Catholic can surely join with good conscience and full heart in the prayers and hymns, listen to the Bible readings and sermon as Christian messages, and contribute to the collection offering. If it is Sunday worship, he need not be scrupulous about missing the services of his own church.

209. Are there times when a Catholic should worship in a non-Catholic church and vice versa?

Surely parties to a mixed marriage should occasionally worship in each other's churches out of respect for the beliefs each holds. Maturely-instructed children of such marriages should also worship occasionally in the church of the spouse in whose faith they are not being reared. Otherise, these children may reach maturity thinking that their mother or father has no religion at all and no say in their religious upbringing.

210. Can a non-Catholic receive holy communion in a Catholic church?

Not as a general rule. Holy communion involves a specific Catholic belief about the "real presence" of Jesus in the bread and wine. If a non-Catholic does not have that belief, he would be acting against his conscience in accepting communion. Granting, however, that he does share belief in the "real presence," he still is not completely one in faith and life with the other communicants. Accepting holy communion under such circumstances would, at the least, put him into a highly ambiguous position. Of what Church is he a communicant?

211.   Could there ever be an exceptional case in which a non-Catholic could receive holy communion in a Catholic service?

Yes, there is. Orthodox Christians are admitted to holy communion at their request. The case of Protestants requesting holy communion is handled a bit more gingerly. Granting that a Protestant personally shares in Catholic belief about the "real presence" of Jesus in the eucharist and granting that he has an urgent spiritual need for holy communion which cannot be served by his own minister, he may receive communion in a Catholic service. The Catholic Church feels that his pressing need outweighs his lack of total agreement in faith and life with the other communicants.

212.   What constitutes the "urgent spiritual need" which permits a Protestant to receive holy communion in a Catholic service?

The cases of persecuted and/or imprisoned Protestants, cut off from their own communion, are universally recognized as "urgent spiritual needs." The logical extension of such cases is left up to conferences of bishops and the local bishop is permitted to extend them to fit local circumstances. One suspects that bishops will interpret "urgent spiritual need" generously, e.g., long-term patients in a convalescent hospital who are not visited by a minister.

213.   Could a Catholic receive holy communion at a non-Catholic service?

With the exception of an Orthodox Mass, he cannot. It is not because Catholics, generally, think that Protestants do not believe in the "real presence" nor is it because Catholics do not have urgent spiritual needs which a minister may legitimately serve. The problem is this: Catholics have always found it difficult to discern how a clergyman ordained as a minister of the gospel has the power to celebrate the eucharist. It is the grave uncertainty as to whether the "real presence" is actually *accomplished* in a Protestant eucharist which divides Catholics and Protestants on the question of intercommunion.

Chapter 10

CHURCH ORGANIZATION

CHURCH TRADITION

214. Is every feature of today's Roman Catholic Church somehow connected with the presence of the risen savior in the world?

Not necessarily. Some features are purely administrative. Determining which features embody the presence of the risen savior involves an inquiry into *tradition*.

215. What is tradition?

Tradition is the Church's search for self-understanding. The search for what is authentic and essential in today's Church involves an inquiry into the teachings of Jesus as lived, preached, and taught by generation after generation of the Christian community.

216. By Church tradition, do you mean doing the same things over and over?

Obviously not. Today's Church is not a carbon copy of the Christian community described in the Acts of the Apostles. What the primitive Christians "handed on" has been rendered explicit as succeeding generations lived the faith. It is very much as if one inherited a family tradition of philanthropy. One would not necessarily live up to that tradition by just supporting the good works of previous generations.

217. If I wanted to get a firm grip on Church tradition, what would I do?

The best grip on Church tradition is the constant, ordinary practice and understanding of generation after generation of Christians as to what their faith is all about. A good catechism, for instance, both records and develops Church tradition.

CHURCH INSTITUTIONS: POPE, COUNCIL, BISHOPS, PASTORS

218. Does the Roman Catholic Church have any formal institutions which determine the sense of Church tradition?

At times, the Roman Catholic Church has to come formally to grips with Church tradition. The most ancient device for so doing is a general council of bishops who inquire into the meaning of the faith and, at times, solemnly determine it. Most recently, there are rare instances where the Pope personally solemnly determines the meaning of the faith after due inquiry into Church tradition.

219. Is the Pope part of what was "handed on" from primitive Christianity?

Today's papacy provides an excellent example of what does and what does not belong to Church tradition. Much of what Popes do today just accrued to the office over the centuries. Moreover, the Roman Catholic Church still suffers from the medieval image of the pope as a feudal lord with the bishops as his vassals. Fortunately, this distortion was corrected by the last general council, Vatican II, in its decree on bishops (Oct. 28, 1965).

220. What is authentic Church tradition about the Pope?

In the gospels, Jesus promises that the community of disciples will not fail (Mt 16:13-2). Peter is singled out as chief witness of Christ's word; Peter, especially, is "unfailable" (Lk 22:32; Jn 21:17). Somehow, the faith of Peter sums up the faith of the disciples. Peter's preeminence is recognized by the infant Church (see Acts, chapters 1.12).

The idea of a *witness-spokesman* is the seed from which the papacy developed. He who succeeded to Peter's position also succeeded to Peter's preeminence.

221. What is the Pope's authority in the Roman Catholic Church?

Papal authority, like all evangelical authority, fulfills a service to the believing community (Mt 18). The Pope's unique service to the Church is as spokesman and witness to its faith and life.

222. Does this mean that when the Pope acts as spokesman-witness he cannot make a mistake?

It took a long time for this idea to crystallize out of Church tradition. But, in 1870, the first Vatican Council solemnly defined this to be the sense of Church tradition. When the Pope, invoking his authority, solemnly and deliberately pronounces on matters of Christian faith and morals, he cannot err. Otherwise, the Church would have failed its Lord.

223. Do you mean that, if the Pope solemnly proclaimed that the earth was flat, every Catholic would have to believe it?

Obviously not. The Pope would be outside his competence in pronouncing on a scientific matter.

224. But can the Pope pronounce infallibly on all matters within his competence?

No, he cannot. Popes do not have private revelations about every facet of Church tradition. Like any other member of the Church, the Pope has to study and inquire carefully into Church tradition in order to pronounce infallibly upon it. His conviction about its sense must be reasoned-out and assured.

225. Does this mean that Roman Catholics need pay no attention to the Pope's everyday statements about religious matters?

The Pope's ordinary, everyday statements about Christian faith and life are the words of one charged with a unique responsibility for the whole Church. A Catholic gives religious assent to such teaching in the belief that it is a safe guide as to the meaning of Church tradition.

226. How often has the Pope made an infallible decision?

Only twice in the history of the Church so far. In both cases, once in 1854, and once in 1950, a Pope solemnly declared the sense of tradition about the special holiness of Mary, the mother of Jesus. Actually, there was no doubt about either case and the Pope chose to honor Catholic belief with a solemn pronouncement.

227. What does the Roman Catholic Church do if Church tradition is unclear?

The usual device for determining tradition in such a case is to call a general council of bishops.

228. What is a general council?

A general or ecumenical council is a meeting to which the bishops of the whole world are summoned to debate and discuss matters affecting Church belief, life, or discipline. Its decisions always need papal approval to have binding force. There have been twenty-one general councils. The first was the Council of Nicaea in 325; the most recent was the second Vatican Council (four sessions, 1962-65).

229. Can a general council render infallible decisions?

Yes, Catholic belief has always been that the Church could not fail its Lord on such a serious occasion. Amusingly enough, this very belief has never itself been defined by a Pope or a council. Catholic belief has just naturally seen the body of bishops as the authentic witness to Church belief and life.

230. Do general councils always render infallible decisions?

No, they do not. Not all councils see the need or the possibility of making infallible decisions. The record is held by the Council of Trent (24 sessions, 1545-63) with over seventy decisions. Vatican II made no infallible decisions but issued various documents summarizing Church tradition at mid-twentieth century. Such documents, of course, have the highest authority.

The bishops during one of the four sessions of the Second Vatican Council at St. Peter's in Rome.

231. Why are only bishops voting members of a general council?

It is because a bishop's office makes him the responsible guardian and teacher of Church tradition. Christ's mandate to the apostles (Mt 28:16-20; Mk 16:15-16) was passed on by them to *episcopoi* (overseers) in the infant communities which the apostles founded. Episcopoi were singled out by the laying on of hands and the invocation of the Holy Spirit as is done yet in the ordination of a bishop. The letters to Timothy and Titus show how this office was conceived in apostolic times.

232. What is the authority of a bishop?

The authority of a bishop, like all evangelical authority, is one of service to the local church (diocese). He serves, basically, to keep the believing community straight or, more technically, *orthodox*.

233. Is an individual bishop infallible in his own diocese?

No, he is not. Tradition sees the individual bishop as the witness to orthodoxy. In order to be orthodox himself, he has to be guided by tradition and learn from it. Bishops may decide doctrine in council; at home, they teach and preach it.

234.   What is the role of the pastor and parish in the Catholic Church?

Pastors and parishes are long-standing Church institutions dating from about the fifth century. They arose when the believing community became too large to be directly served by the bishop and his associated priests. However, if parishes were someday found to work against good church life, they could be abolished.

235.   What is a Catholic's relation to his parish?

This relation is determined by church law. Present law in the Latin rite of the Catholic Church automatically identifies a Catholic with the territorial parish in which he resides unless he belongs to a special group, e.g., servicemen. A parishioner is expected to identify himself to his pastor and contribute to the maintenance of the parish.

The floating Catholic who never identifies himself to his pastor and who surfaces only for necessary pastoral care, usually in emergencies, is the bane of the parish priest's existence. Such a Catholic misses something of what it means to belong to a believing community if he does not share in his parish's day-to-day life.

236.   May a Catholic never go to any church except his parish church?

Catholics have the right to attend Mass and, with some restrictions, receive the sacraments in any Catholic church or chapel of any rite. Present law makes *baptism* and *marriage* a parish affair. Without the pastor's permission, a child may not be baptized nor a couple be married outside the (bride's) parish. (The baptism and marriage would be valid; but the priest who performed either would be subject to reproof.) *Funerals* usually take place in the parish church of the deceased unless he requested another church.

All this is the law. But parish churches are not mere conveniences like service-stations. They are communities and, like all communities, are weakened if the parishioners have no particular loyalty to them.

Chapter 11

THE CHURCH AT WORSHIP

LITURGY

237. What is liturgy?

Liturgy is the public and official ritual whereby the Church worships the Father in and through its union with the risen savior. Some liturgical rituals are prayers, some are actions.

238. What is the liturgical prayer of the Catholic Church?

The Church's liturgical prayer is called the divine office (*officium* - duty). It consists of psalms, readings, and prayers which are said at specified times during the day. (Hence, it is also called the liturgy of the hours.) Monks and nuns in solemn vows are obliged to say the office together in their monastery or convent. Catholic clergy (bishops, priests, and deacons) say the divine office privately.

239. Are the many devotions found in Catholic prayer books also liturgical prayer?

No, they are not. Such devotions grew out of everyday piety. Some devotions are encouraged by Church authority because they are especially authentic expressions of Catholic belief and life. All devotions are subject to approval by Church authority. That is why books of Catholic devotions must carry the *imprimatur* of a bishop. The *imprimatur* means that the book contains nothing harmful or erroneous. It does not mean that the bishop positively recommends the book.

240. What are the liturgical actions of the Catholic Church?

In order of importance, first comes the eucharist or Mass and the administration of the sacraments. Great care is taken that the ritual surrounding these is in accord with Church tradition. Finally, there is the invocation of blessings on persons as well as on things which serve human needs. Such blessings are instituted or approved by Church authorities.

241. Why do Catholics call the Lord's Supper the "eucharist" or the "Mass"?

"The Lord's Supper" is surely the most ancient name (1 Cor 11:20). At the Last Supper, Jesus "rendered thanks" (*eucharistein*) for the bread and wine. Thus, "eucharist" became a name for the ritual. "Mass" is the result of an amusing misunderstanding. In the Latin rite, the eucharist concludes with a dismissal *(missa)*. Non-Latin speaking peoples thought that *missa* was the name for the whole ceremony.

242. Isn't there also a liturgical year?

Yes, there are special liturgical seasons, days of festivity, and days of penance. Most American parishes provide their members with a calendar of the liturgical year. An appendix to this lesson outlines the liturgical year.

SUNDAY MASS

243. What is the most important liturgical day?

Sunday is the most important liturgical day. Every Sunday commemorates that first day of the week on which Christ rose from death. Present Church law obliges Catholics to attend Mass every Sunday and to abstain from needless work and business (canon 1247). Liturgically, Sundays and all great feasts begin at sunset of the previous day. That is why Catholics can attend Sunday Mass on Saturday evening.

244. What is the point of this strict Church law on Sunday worship?

Theologians point out that the Sunday "obligation" points both backward and forward. The Christian *remembers* the freedom from toil of the Old Testament sabbath and the freedom from sin won by Christ. The Christian *awaits* the world-to-come in which sheer toil and sheer busyness will come to an end. Sunday makes a space-in-life for the Christian to express these beliefs. Church law insists that this space be made, week by week, in the believer's life.

245. Is it seriously wrong to miss Sunday Mass?

Yes, there is a serious obligation imposed by Church law. But Church law, like any human law, gives way in the face of physical impossibility or a higher duty. One who is ill or one whose services are essentially needed is excused from Sunday Mass. So, too, one who usually attends Sunday Mass is surely excused occasionally if needed rest or relaxation makes it highly inconvenient to get to church.

246. How can a non-Catholic learn to follow the ceremonies of the Mass?

The best way is to follow the Mass with a Mass-book (missal) of some sort. If you can have a Catholic friend along to prompt you, all the better. Every congregation has some naturally slow people so no one will notice if you fall behind or get lost. An appendix to this lesson outlines the basic etiquette of the Mass.

247. More importantly, how can one understand the meaning of the eucharistic part of the Mass?

The meaning of the eucharistic part of the Mass has called forth some of the deepest theological reflection in Church tradition. To understand the eucharist, you have to understand it as both *sacrifice* and *sacrament*.

THE MASS: A SACRIFICE

248. What is a sacrifice?

In a sacrifice, something is dedicated to God. If the sacrifice is not physically destroyed as a sign of its dedication, it is often partaken of by those offering the sacrifice. The partaking makes them holy and acceptable to the divinity.

249.   Is the eucharist a sacrifice?

Yes, it is. At the Last Supper, Jesus took bread and wine and identified his body and blood with them. Specifically, he identified his body and blood about to be given in sacrifice on Golgotha with the eucharistic bread and wine. Every Mass repeats this action of Jesus. Those who partake of the eucharistic bread and wine in holy communion are sanctified by sharing in the very obedient love of Jesus, the love which reconciled the whole world to the heavenly Father.

250.   Can the eucharist be anything but a symbolic sacrifice unless Jesus himself is really present by the bread and wine?

At the Last Supper, the intent of Jesus to institute a genuine sacrifice is obvious. There is nothing symbolic about his words. But the actual sacrifice of Jesus could not be shared in by a communicant unless Jesus himself is present by the bread and wine of the eucharist. Thus, the bread does more than symbolize Jesus' body; it really is that body-given. So, too, the wine does more than symbolize Jesus' blood; it really is that blood-shed.

HOW JESUS IS PRESENT IN THE EUCHARIST

251.   How is Jesus present in the eucharist?

The body and blood of Jesus are present in the eucharist by transubstantiation. This is the term chosen by the Council of Trent (session 13, Oct. 11, 1551) to define Catholic belief.

252.   What did the Council of Trent mean by transubstantiation?

Transubstantiation means that the very stuff of bread becomes the body-given and the very stuff of wine becomes the blood-shed of Christ. Jesus, therefore, is present in the eucharist by a change wrought in the bread and wine, *not* by a change wrought in himself. The doctrine states that the presence of Christ is real. But the doctrine denies that the physical body and blood of the risen Lord are, somehow, conveyed from glory into the bread and wine.

253. Did the Council of Trent mean that the eucharistic bread and wine are, somehow, physically different from ordinary bread and wine?

The Council of Trent was totally innocent of physics. They had in mind a *conversion-process.* The physical properties of bread and wine remain unaltered but, on another plane of reality, the real presence of the body and blood of Christ is accomplished. What changes is the *place* of this bread and wine in the whole scheme of things. Putting it more technically, the substance or nature of bread and wine is converted into a real presence of Christ's body and blood.

THE MASS: A SACRAMENT

254. How does Christ become present in the eucharist?

Christ's eucharistic presence is accomplished by the words of institution (consecration) pronounced by an ordained priest acting in and for the Church. This ritual *accomplishes* what it signifies. It is a sacrament.

"Do this in remembrance of me" (Lk 22:10).

255. What is a sacrament?

A sacrament is a visible ritual, rooted in Jesus' institution of the Church, which conveys Jesus' saving actions to the believer. The more classical definition is: A sacrament is a sacred sign, instituted by Christ, to give grace.

256. Is it the priest's words which actually accomplish the eucharistic presence of Jesus?

Indeed, they do. Sacraments do what they say. The words of institution define precisely what this bread and wine become at Mass.

257. What does it add to our understanding of the eucharist to know that the presence of Jesus is accomplished by a sacrament?

If sacraments *do* what they say, then the words of institution make Jesus present in a way mysteriously identical with his actual sacrifice on Golgotha. Putting it crudely, the eucharistic presence is not just any old body and any old blood of Jesus. The words of institution define the eucharistic bread and wine as the sacrificed body and blood of Jesus. Thus, the eucharist proclaims the death of the Lord (see 1 Cor 11:26).

258. Does the Mass, somehow, make Jesus' death on Golgotha happen again?

No, it does not. Christ died, once and for all, for our sins (Heb 9:25ff). Protestants, rightly, have rejected incautious Catholic statements which make the Mass a recurrence or a too-literal re-enactment of the actual death of Jesus.

259. If Jesus' dying isn't actually present in the Mass, how can the Mass be a genuine sacrifice?

Jesus' actual death is not present or in any way re-enacted at Mass. Nothing of this need be the case in order for the Mass to be a genuine sacrifice. What is present in the eucharist is the same Jesus whose humanity is forever dedicated to the salvation of humankind. The Church's sacrifice is the ever-dedicated savior present in symbols which sacramentally recall his death on Golgotha.

260. How is the Mass an actual sacrifice?

The words of institution are spoken over *two* things, bread and wine. Besides being the vehicles of holy communion, the bread and wine also *recall* something about Jesus. They memorialize the time when Jesus' body was actually given and his blood actually shed on Golgotha.

261. How does the fact that the eucharistic bread and wine recall and memorialize Jesus' actual death make the Mass an actual sacrifice?

The eucharistic bread and wine are not merely a memorial of what once was. By them, the same savior, now our risen

Lord, is really present to this congregation *with the same dedication* to us as he had at his dying. At Mass, the memorial of Jesus' dying consists in the sacramental realities of the separately consecrated bread and wine; and the dedication is everlastingly present wherever Jesus is present. That sacrificial dedication merits the same everlasting response from the heavenly Father. At Mass, the Father's response is to this congregation and to all who are remembered or share in its act of worship.

THE REAL PRESENCE

"Eat this bread and drink this cup" (1 Cor 11:26)

262. Why say a "real presence of Christ's body and blood"? Why not say that the eucharist contains Christ's body and blood?

The eucharist does contain the risen, physical Christ whose body and blood are forever united to his divine person. However, the word "contain" could connote a spatial presence like the presence our bodies have in the universe. There is but one such spatial presence of Christ: he exists in eternal glory with the Father. The eucharist does not duplicate that presence. The eucharistic presence simply has no counterpart.

263. Are there any practical consequences to knowing that the eucharistic presence of Jesus is not a duplicating of his spatial presence in heaven?

Yes, there are. Believers have been upset and even repelled by incautious statements about "really" eating the body of Jesus and "really" drinking his blood in holy communion. Such statements are not correct. One eats the eucharistic bread and drinks the eucharistic wine. Nothing whatever is physically happening to Christ. Rather, something spiritual is happening to the communicant. What it is, will be suggested in the next two questions.

264. What, precisely, about the bread and wine is altered in the conversion process?

No doctrinal definition exists on this point except that the alteration is real, i.e., independent of one's thinking or feeling about the eucharist. A consideration of bread and wine might lead to the conclusion that their substance consists in the food and drink into which wheat and grapes have been made. Thus, a change in their very substance may be a complete conversion of a natural food and drink into something totally different.

265. What is illuminating about considering the conversion process as a total transformation of the eucharistic bread and wine precisely as food and drink?

If this be so, then the real presence of Jesus in the eucharist would be a dynamic one. Once holy communion has been received and Jesus has entered into the communicant, his very presence would be meant to nourish and refresh the communicant on his pilgrim way to the kingdom of God. Jesus himself is the communicant's food and drink unto life eternal (see Jn 6:53ff.).

266. Do any Church practices support the opinion that the conversion-process lies in the food-value and drink-value of the eucharistic bread and wine?

Yes, some Church practices support this opinion. For instance, a crumb of sacramental bread too small to eat or a drop of sacramental wine too small to drink is reverently disposed of with no thought that it is a vehicle of the eucharistic presence of Jesus. What cannot nourish or what cannot refresh also cannot contain the eucharistic presence.

267. Is the eucharistic presence a presence of Jesus' very self?

The eucharistic presence is a presence of Jesus' very self, risen from death, and forever forming a living whole with his body and blood. It is that glorious body and that glorious blood which are present in the eucharistic bread and wine.

268. Does this doctrine of the presence of the person of Jesus in either the eucharistic bread or the eucharistic wine explain why Catholics of the Latin rite generally receive only the eucharistic bread in holy communion?

It does partly. For roughly the last five centuries, only the eucharistic bread has been given in communion to Latin-rite faithful. Large crowds of communicants made it practical. Then, too, there was a sort of theological reason. John Hus (1369?-1415) denied that this sort of communion was sufficient and the Catholic Church rejected his teaching.

269. What is the point of Jesus' command to eat and drink?

The command has to do with what Jesus wills to accomplish in the communicant. He wills the salvation accomplished in his body and by his blood to be both nourishment and refreshment to believers. Just as in ordinary life we need both, so it is in the life of the spirit. Fortunately, the Latin rite is restoring communion under both kinds.

HOLY COMMUNION

270. Why did Jesus choose bread and wine for the eucharist?

Bread and wine have a universal symbolism because they are the simplest and most common forms of nourishment and refreshment. Perhaps, then, Jesus wants to indicate how accessible he wishes to be in holy communion.

271. What does holy communion accomplish?

Holy communion is the means by which Jesus shares with his disciples his personal sacrifice and his personal victory over sin and death. By the bread and wine of the eucharist, the ever-dedicated redeemer who is the Holy One of God, sanctifies the lives of those who believe in him.

272. Is nourishing and refreshing the individual communicant the sole purpose of holy communion?

No, it is not. Many believers are communicants in the one Lord. Their community in discipleship is strengthened by communion. Even more, their share in Jesus' sacrifice and victory is a pledge of its final fulfillment, with him, in the world-to-come. The whole Church grows in holiness and hope by the eucharist.

273. What spiritual conditions are necessary to receive holy communion?

To receive holy communion worthily, one must be free of serious sin, have a sufficient understanding of Jesus' presence in the eucharist, and have a worthy motive for receiving. A worthy motive is presumed in someone who has participated in the Mass to the best of his ability. Sufficient understanding of Jesus' presence in the eucharist is presumed to exist by age seven. Church law (canon 916) demands that one who has committed serious sin, although he has personally repented, receive the sacrament of penance before receiving communion, unless a grave reason is present and there is no opportunity of confessing.

274. What bodily conditions are necessary to receive holy communion?

The bodily conditions necessary to receive holy communion are at least a one-hour fast from food and nourshing drink. Water and medicine do not break the communion fast. The hour is computed from the time of communion, not from the beginning of Mass. The sick and the aged, and those who attend them, are not obliged to this fast (canon 919).

275. How is holy communion received?

Communicants sometimes kneel at the sanctuary rail but, more often, they stand before the one distributing. If they wish to receive the communion bread in the hand, they cup their out-stretched hands, left hand over right. If they wish to receive on the tongue, they keep their hands folded.

The distributor says: "The body of Christ" and the communicant responds "Amen." Then the communicant who wishes to receive in the hand is given the eucharistic bread in his cupped left hand and, after a step to the side, communicates himself with his right hand. The communicant who wishes to receive on the tongue opens his mouth and extends his tongue slightly over his lower lip so that the distributor may place the communion bread on his tongue. It is perfectly proper to chew the eucharistic bread and also perfectly proper to move away immediately to make room for another communicant.

If the eucharistic wine is also being received, the distributor says: "The blood of Christ" and the communicant responds "Amen." Then the communicant accepts the chalice (cup) from the distributor and takes a sip of the communion wine.

At times, communion is distributed by intinction (dipping). The distributor dips the communion bread into the wine and says: "The body and blood of Christ" to which the communicant responds "Amen." Then the communicant receives the dipped eucharistic bread on his extended tongue.

276. How often must a Catholic receive holy communion?

Jesus' command to eat his body and drink his blood does not specify the frequency of holy communion. Surely, though, his command implies that holy communion is a normal part of Church worship and not some sort of reward for special virtue. Church law has specified the absolute *minimum* frequency of holy communion:

a) Holy Communion must be received by a person facing the danger of death from any cause, even external circumstances of special hazard (canon 921).

b) Holy communion must be received once a year during the Easter season (canon 920). In the United States, the Easter season runs from the first Sunday of Lent to Trinity Sunday (the Sunday after Pentecost).

277. How often may a Catholic receive holy communion?

Holy communion may be received daily at a parish Mass. It may also be received again at another parish Mass at which the communicant *participates*, i.e., not a Mass at which the communicant is present while just prolonging his prayers from a previous Mass. In addition, if the communicant participates in a Mass celebrated for another purpose, such as a baptism, wedding or funeral, he may receive communion again that day.

278. What kind of bread and wine are used for the eucharist?

In the Latin rite, unleavened wheat bread and pure grape wine are used. The eastern rites also use grape wine but use a rather heavy, leavened wheat bread. Currently, in the Latin rite, there is more and more insistence that the unleavened bread truly have the look and consistency of bread, and not be a mere wafer which melts in one's mouth. In cases of real necessity, any wheat bread and any grape wine could be used.

279. Can someone be given a special remembrance at Mass?

Yes, Mass is "said" for someone's intentions at his request. Custom has attached a donation (stipend) for the priest's support to such a remembrance. By Church law, bishops and pastors must say Mass on Sundays and holydays for their flocks. They may not accept any stipend for these obligatory Masses.

EUCHARISTIC DEVOTION

280. Is any of the consecrated eucharist reserved in the church outside of Mass?

Yes, from earliest times the consecrated eucharistic bread was retained for communion of the sick. Out of this reservation grew the various devotions to the eucharistic presence of Jesus outside of Mass. Presently, in churches of the Latin rite, the consecrated bread is retained in a structure called a tabernacle.

281. Where is the tabernacle in a Catholic church?

Sometimes, the tabernacle is a free-standing structure; sometimes it is built into a wall or an altar. The tabernacle is usually located on a shelf or altar on the back wall of the church or in a side chapel. The tabernacle can be identified by the veil which covers it and the lamp burning before or beside it.

During Benediction, the priest makes the sign of the cross over the people with the monstrance holding the Eucharistic Lord.

282. What forms of devotion to the eucharistic presence of Jesus in the tabernacle have arisen in the Catholic Church?

The faithful have recognized a specific presence of Jesus to his Church in the reserved eucharist. In the tabernacle is the Lord and savior, still the humble servant of his disciples as their food unto everlasting life. This presence of Lord-and-servant lies at the center of all eucharistic devotions.

283. What form does private, personal devotion to the eucharistic presence of Jesus in the tabernacle take?

Private, personal prayer before the tabernacle takes the form of a *communing* with the savior modeled upon the actual reception of holy communion. Catholics often speak of such devotion as a "visit" to the blessed sacrament.

284. What form does public, group devotion to the eucharistic presence of Jesus in the tabernacle take?

Public, group devotion to the eucharistic presence emphasizes the lordship of Jesus. In the service called *Benediction*, the sacrament is exposed for public worship in a special vessel which makes the consecrated bread visible and, at the conclusion of the service, the worshipers are blessed with the sacrament.

There is also a solemn exposition of the sacrament in the same vessel known as *Forty Hours*. This time of worship (originally forty hours in length) involves periods of private prayer, public devotion, and concludes with Benediction. Many dioceses have it so arranged that churches take turns throughout the year in conducting this devotion.

APPENDIX I: THE LITURGICAL YEAR

The liturgical year begins with *Advent* on the fourth Sunday before Christmas. Advent is a season of prayerful preparation remembering the coming of Jesus in the flesh and preparing for his coming in glory. Violet vestments are used for the seasonal Masses.

Then follows the *Christmas* season, from December 25 to January 13. The Christmas season commemorates the manifestations of Jesus, from his birth to the early manifestations of his messiahship. White vestments are used for the seasonal Masses. This is followed by a variable ordinary period until *Lent* begins on Ash Wednesday.

Lent is a forty-six day period of preparation for Easter. It is a period of penance and spiritual renewal in anticipation of the greatest feast of the year, Easter. Violet vestments are used for the seasonal Masses.

Lent ends with *Holy Week* during which the actual events of Jesus' passion and death are commemorated, especially on Holy Thursday and Good Friday. The Saturday before Easter is the only non-liturgical day of the year.

The *Easter* season begins on Holy Saturday evening with the great Easter vigil and lasts for fifty days, ending with the feast of Pentecost. This season commemorates the risen Lord and the founding of the Church. White vestments are used for the seasonal Masses, except for Pentecost, when red is used to commemorate the tongues of fire by which the Holy Spirit manifested Himself.

After Pentecost, the *ordinary season* resumes with the Sunday next due from before Lent. There are thirty-four ordinary Sundays in the liturgical year which fill the gap between Christmas and Lent and the gap between Pentecost and Advent. The ordinary season is devoted to lessons in Christian living. Green vestments are used for the seasonal Masses.

Scattered throughout the liturgical year are special *feasts* in honor of Christ or Mary or the saints. Usually, white vestments are worn on such feasts. Red, however, is used on feasts which commemorate the passion of Jesus or the death of a martyr-saint.

Some feasts are *holy days*. Like Sundays, Mass must be attended on holy days. In the United States, the following feasts are holy days:

Immaculate Conception of Mary	— December 8
Christmas Day	— December 25
Solemnity of Mary, Mother of God	— January 1
Ascension Day	— Thursday, 40 days after Easter
Assumption of Mary into Heaven	— August 15
Feast of All Saints	— November 1

Some days are days of *penance*. In the United States, they are:

Ash Wednesday and Good Friday — days of fast for anyone over twenty-one and not yet fifty-nine. No meat and only one full meal. Two other light meals which, together, do not add up to another full meal may be eaten.

Ash Wednesday and all Fridays of Lent — days of abstinence for anyone over fourteen. No meat.

Fridays outside Lent and all weekdays of Lent — personal penance for everyone. No meat recommended for non-Lenten Fridays.

APPENDIX II: CHURCH ETIQUETTE AT MASS

When you enter the church, the first thing to look for is the *holy water font*. It is located adjacent to the door, roughly waist-high. It contains blessed water as a reminder of baptism.

You go to the font, dip the tips of the middle fingers of your right hand in the water, and make the *sign of the cross*. This is done by touching the middle fingers of your right hand to forehead, breastbone, left shoulder, and right shoulder. While doing this, you say quietly: "In the name of the Father, and of the Son, and of the Holy Spirit. Amen." The sign of the cross is the prayer with which all Catholic services and devotions begin.

When you reach the pew you have chosen, you *genuflect* toward the tabernacle before you enter the pew. A genuflection is made by bending the right knee until it touches the floor. If the genuflection is done gracefully, one's right knee will be next to one's left ankle. Most Catholics hold on to the end of the pew while genuflecting; it avoids an unexpected sprawl in the church aisle.

Pews in Catholic churches have kneeling benches lying in wait for unwary ankles. So be careful when you enter the pew. If the kneeling bench is tipped up out of the way, it should be lowered so one can *kneel* for a moment of private prayer. Then you may be seated if you wish.

When you enter the church for private devotion, you follow the same etiquette: holy water, sign of the cross, genuflection, and kneeling for private prayer. If you happen to move from one side of the church to the other, you genuflect toward the tabernacle if you pass directly in front of it.

Most churches have some sort of Mass-book (missal or missalette) available in the pews. This contains the formula for the Mass. Some parts of the Mass are the same always; some parts of the Mass vary everyday. For instance, you may open a missalette and find yourself confronted with a half-dozen sets of Bible readings. Only one of these sets, the one proper to the day, will be used at Mass. So if you find yourself hearing a prayer or reading which you do not see on the page, look further on. One hopes it will be there somewhere.

Remember, too, that such things as invitations to prayer or penitence may be improvised by the priest. Thus, the missalette may simply say "let us pray" and the priest may elaborate upon it. Don't think you have lost your place unless the next thing which is said has no relation to what is on the page in front of you. If that happens, you have lost your place. A discreet look at the book of the person next to you may be in order.

Sacred hymns emphasize the celebration-character of the Eucharist.

Then, too, if hymns are sung, certain spoken parts of the Mass are omitted or are said quietly by the priest. It can be very baffling to open a missalette, find a whole page of entrance antiphons, or communion antiphons, and miss the direction that these are not said if an entrance or a communion hymn is sung. Likewise, if a hymn is sung during the preparation of the bread and wine, the prayers of blessing are said quietly by the priest.

A standard Sunday Mass goes something like this: After opening announcements are made to clue the congregation on what Mass formula is going to be used, the congregation rises to sing the entrance hymn. During the hymn, the celebrant of the Mass enters. When he reaches the sanctuary, he greets the congregation. The standard response to whatever greeting he uses is: "And also with you."

Next the celebrant invites the congregation to penitence and a brief period of silence follows. The priest then leads the congregation in a prayer of penitence. He will use one of three formulas. If what he is saying seems to have no relation to what is on the page, he is improvising on the third formula. Next comes the prayer of praise "Glory to God in the highest." It can be said or sung. This prayer is omitted on the Sundays of Advent and Lent.

Then the priest says or sings the opening prayer of the Mass. This prayer is different for every Sunday of the year.

The congregation is now seated for the service or liturgy of the Word. This, too, is different for every Sunday of the year. There is a first reading, a responsorial psalm, and a second reading. At times, the psalm between the readings may be replaced by a vocal or instrumental solo or even a period of reflective silence.

After the second reading, the congregation rises to hear the words of the gospel. This reading is introduced by an acclamation. Except during Lent, it is an "Alleluia" and a verse which may be elaborately sung. As the priest introduces the gospel, you will notice him making a triple sign of the cross with his thumb on forehead, lips, and breastbone. This same triple sign of the cross is made by the congregation.

After the gospel, the congregation is seated for the homily or sermon. Announcements may also be made at this time.

After the sermon, the congregation rises for the profession of faith which is introduced either by the priest or a leader. Following the profession of faith, a series of intercessory prayers called "prayers of the faithful" is said. Extreme freedom is allowed in improvising these prayers so you must listen to each petition. The petitions customarily end with "we pray to the Lord" or "let us pray to the Lord." The usual response is: "Lord, hear our prayer." The intercessions conclude with a prayer led by the priest to which the response is "Amen."

Then the congregation is seated and preparations for the eucharistic part of the Mass begin. The collection is taken up, the bread and wine are brought to the altar, and prayers of blessing are said over each. A hymn may be sung during all or part of this "preparation of the gifts." Sometimes, it all goes on at once.

More often, though, the collection is taken up first. Then a hymn is announced. As the hymn is being sung, the bread and wine and the collection are taken to the sanctuary in a procession. As the hymn continues, the priest says the prayers of blessing quietly. When the hymn concludes, the priest says an elaborate invitation to prayer to which the congregation makes an equally elaborate response: "May the Lord accept this sacrifice at your hands. . . ."

Then the congregation rises for the prayer over the gifts which is different for every Sunday. At the conclusion of this prayer, the priest begins the dialogue which introduces the Preface to the eucharistic prayer. The priest then continues saying or singing the Preface. Usually, a missalette will not print the Preface since the priest may choose from so many.

At the end of the Preface, the congregation responds by saying or singing the acclamation "Holy, holy, holy. . . ." Then, in the United States, it is customary to kneel for the whole eucharistic prayer even though the official directions assume that the congregation will stand after the words of institution.

The priest will use one of four eucharistic prayers. If he himself does not announce which one he is using, each prayer can be recognized by its different opening words. Inserted in each eucharistic prayer are the words of institution (consecration) pronounced first over the bread and then the wine. After the words of instittuion are pronounced over the bread, the priest will pause briefly to show the eucharistic bread for the congregation's worship. He will do the same with the eucharistic wine. By custom, a tiny bell may be rung at both moments to call this act to the attention of the congregation.

After the consecration of the bread and wine, the priest invites the congregation to proclaim the "mystery of faith." The congregation responds by saying or singing one of four acclamations as they are directed. The eucharistic prayer then continues.

The eucharistic prayer concludes with the elevation of the eucharistic bread and wine while the priest says or sings the prayer of praise: "Through him, with him, and in him, all honor and glory is Yours, almighty Father, forever and ever." The congregation responds by saying or singing the great "Amen."

Then the congregation rises to begin the preparation for communion. The priest begins with an invitation to prayer and the congregation responds by saying or singing the "Our Father." The priest continues by elaborating formally on the last petition of the Lord's prayer with "Deliver us, Lord, from every evil. . . ." At the end of his prayer, the congregation responds "For the kingdom, the power, and the glory are yours, now and forever."

This is followed by a prayer for Christ's peace and the priest's wish for that peace: "The peace of the Lord be with you always." To his greeting, the congregation responds: "And also with you." At the discretion of the priest, the congregation may be invited to exchange a wish of peace. If you are so invited, you turn to your neighbor, offer him your hand, and wish him the Lord's peace.

The priest now proceeds to break the large altar-bread. While he does so, the congregation says or sings the threefold "Lamb of God. . . ." After this, in some places, the congregation will kneel as the priest privately prepares for his own communion.

When the priest has finished his private preparation, he elevates the eucharistic bread and announces: "This is the Lamb of God. . . ." The congregation responds: "Lord, I am not worthy. . . ." While the priest receives his own communion, a communion hymn may be announced. Those in the congregation who wish to receive holy communion now come forward, receive, and return to their places. Non-communicants make room for them to enter and leave their pews. After holy communion is distributed, a meditative interlude may follow. The congregation is seated, an instrumental or vocal solo may occur, or silence may be observed. At the end of this period, the congregation rises for the prayer after communion which varies for every Sunday. Announcements may follow this prayer.

Finally, there is the rite of dismissal. The priest greets the congregation, then blesses them with either a simple or an elaborate formula to which response is "Amen." Then he concludes with a dismissal to which the response is "Thanks be to God."

A concluding hymn may be sung during which the priest leaves the sanctuary. At the end of the hymn, you may leave or remain for private prayer. If you are leaving along with a large congregation, it is proper to genuflect in your pew so as not to block the aisle. Making the sign of the cross with holy water before you go out of the door is customary, even if not quite appropriate just after you have been blessed.

Chapter 12

THE SACRAMENTS

WHAT A SACRAMENT IS

285. What is a sacrament?

A sacrament is a visible ritual, rooted in Jesus' institution of the Church, which transmits his saving actions to the believer. The classical definition is: A sacrament is a sacred sign, instituted by Christ, to give grace.

286. What is the purpose of sacraments?

Sacraments, so to speak, pinpoint a specific presence of the risen Lord in and to his Church. They create a continuity of life between today's disciple and Jesus. The Church is meant to do now for believers what Jesus personally did for the first disciples.

Baptism and confirmation are the way today's disciples are called to faith and gifted to live it. Reconciliation of penitents and the anointing of the sick are now the way disciples are reassured when afflicted by moral or physical evil. Matrimony and holy orders are the way the faithful are given special callings to witness Christ's presence in the Church and in the world. Thus, the sacraments give visible assurance that Jesus' mission still goes on.

287. Why is a sacrament a visible ritual?

Jesus himself used significant words and gestures when he worked his wonders of compassion. The Church, following his example, celebrates the wonders of grace in words and actions significant of what is being wrought in the person who receives the sacraments in faith.

288. Did Jesus personally determine the ritual of every sacrament?

It seems not. Jesus certainly gave the example for the eucharist and Matthew (28:19) records a very early baptismal formula. What seems more likely is that the infant Church used either examples or remembered gestures of Jesus to carry on his mission in all confidence that his saving actions would be accomplished by them. Thus, today, aside from the eucharist and baptism, there is considerable divergence in the ritual of the sacraments among the various rites of the Catholic Church.

SACRAMENTS AS CELEBRATIONS

289. Are sacraments just mere rituals?

They are certainly not meant to be—that is, if by "ritual" one means a ceremony which has become devoid of all meaning. The sacraments are rituals in the sense of ceremonial celebrations of the significant events of life. The sacraments celebrate comparable events in the life of the Church.

290. Are sacraments mere ceremonial celebrations of events in the life of the Church?

The sacraments are no more sheerly ceremonial than a genuinely meant birthday present is an empty gesture. Formal expressions, it is true, can become empty gestures if their human meaning is gone. So, too, sacraments could become sheer ceremony if they are not expressions of faith.

291. Are sacraments just celebrations of moments of intense faith?

No, sacraments are more than that. Moments of intense faith can find expression in an indefinite variety of ways which may be meaningful only intermittently and, perhaps, meaningful only to the person experiencing them. The fact that the rituals for the sacraments are part of liturgy and the fact that the celebrations of the sacraments presuppose the presence of a congregation suggests that there is something objective, almost impersonal, going on. Sacraments do more than just express something; they themselves create something. They make Jesus' saving actions present.

SACRAMENTAL GRACE

292. Do sacraments literally make Jesus' saving actions present in the Church?

Yes, they do. Sacraments *themselves* grace their recipients. They are not mere prayers or blessings. Just as Jesus' words or gestures themselves accomplished what they signified, so the sacraments themselves accomplish what they signify. For example, just as Jesus' call to the first disciples itself graced them to follow him, so baptism today accomplishes the grace of Christian commitment.

293. If each of the sacraments graces the recipient, couldn't any sacrament do the job of any other sacrament?

No. Sacraments do what the ritual signifies. Each sacrament brings the saving power of the risen Lord to bear upon a different need in the believer as his life begins and progresses in the Church. Grace, of course, is really a *relation* between the heavenly Father and the recipient brought about by the saving actions of Jesus. This relation is "shaped" differently in each sacrament.

294. Could you give an example of the "shaped" grace of a sacrament?

The best way to discern the way one's relation to the heavenly Father is "shaped" in a sacrament is to study the ritual of its celebration. For instance, the ritual of reconciliation of penitents shows that the recipient is being restored to the life of the Church by the power of the risen Jesus.

295. Is the "shaped" grace of a sacrament the same for each recipient?

No, it is not. It depends on the motives and dispositions of the recipient. One could even commit the sin of sacrilege by receiving a sacrament as an empty, purely ceremonial gesture.

SACRAMENTAL WORTHINESS

296. What are worthy motives and dispositions for receiving a sacrament?

Practically speaking, one who participates in the ritual to the best of his ability is being worthily motivated and worthily disposed to receive the sacrament. Personal reflection and prayer, inspired by a pondering of the ritual, will surely enrich a recipient's sacramental meeting with the saving power of Jesus.

297. Is worthiness ever presumed on the part of the recipient of a sacrament?

Yes, it is. For instance, the anointing of the sick is conferred upon an unconscious person if any presumption exists of his desire to receive it. Generally speaking, the Church presumes worthiness in even its weakest members if they request a sacrament.

298. Would it be unworthy to receive a sacrament if one is not in a mood to receive it?

It would not be unworthy at all. Distinguish between motives and moods. Sacraments are key *events* of the life of faith; they may or may not also be key experiences in the life of faith. Obviously, a key experience in ordinary life would be meaningless if one is not in a mood to appreciate it. But, even in ordinary life, one may securely approach a key event even though one's mood to do so may have disappeared. Many a husband and wife will testify that they were in no mood to get married when their wedding day arrived. Yet they meant what they said.

299.   But doesn't one have to be in the right mood to celebrate anything, even a sacrament?

It all depends on what one means by "celebrate." Sacraments are celebrations of the Church's awe and wonder in the face of God's grace in the person of the risen Christ. If one approaches a sacrament devoid of any sensitivity to this, he is perilously close to sacrilege. But the celebration of a sacrament need not be devised so as to produce the excitement and euphoria of a party. Indeed, the restraint and soberness of the sacramental rituals suggest that too much emotionalism can obscure the sacrament as an event in the life of faith.

SACRAMENTAL RITUAL

300.   What ritual is followed in celebrating a sacrament?

All the sacraments, except reconciliation of penitents, can be conferred after the Liturgy of the Word at Mass. If this cannot be done, a simple Liturgy of the Word is used. The purpose of the service is to effect the framework of faith in which a sacrament is celebrated. After the sacrament is conferred, appropriate prayers or blessings are often added. These are meant to express the Church's sense of the specially graced relationship to the heavenly Father which the sacrament has created in the recipient.

301.   Is the usual ritual ever dispensed with?

In case of urgency, any sacrament is administered immediately without ceremony. An obvious example would be the emergency conferral of the anointing of the sick on a person who was close to death.

302.   Is there any special sequence in which sacraments are celebrated?

Obviously, baptism is always the first sacrament to be received. In any sequence of sacraments, the eucharist always comes last. It is the "last sacrament," even for the dying.

NUMBER AND CLASSIFICATION OF THE SACRAMENTS

303. What events in the life of faith do the sacraments celebrate?

Determining this amounts to determining how many sacraments there are. No one really asked this question until the Protestant Reformation. Until then, the Church celebrated many forms of liturgy with an awareness that some were sacramental and some were not. After searching tradition, the Council of Trent (March 3, 1547) solemnly defined the matter. There are only *seven* sacraments: baptism, confirmation, reconciliation of penitents, holy eucharist, anointing of the sick, holy orders and matrimony.

304. How are the seven sacraments classified?

No pattern or grouping of the seven sacraments has been defined as doctrine. How one classifies the sacraments depends on what one has in mind about the life of faith. For example, three sacraments—baptism, confirmation, and holy orders— confer a permanent status (character) in the Church and, thus, are never repeated.

Looking at it from another angle, three of the sacraments— baptism, reconciliation of penitents, and anointing of the sick —have to do with sin and its consequences. Another way of classifying the sacraments is to look at each sacrament as contributing to form a graced community worthy to celebrate the greatest of the sacraments, namely, the eucharist.

305. Is there a convenient way of grouping the sacraments for purposes of teaching?

Leaving aside the eucharist, which is unique, there is a convenient way of teaching the sacraments in pairs:

a) Sacraments of initiation, namely, baptism and confirmation.

b) Sacraments of crisis, namely, reconciliation of penitents and anointing of the sick.

c) Sacraments of vocation, namely, holy orders and matrimony.

Chapter 13

SACRAMENTS OF INITIATION

BAPTISM

306. Why are baptism and confirmation called sacraments of initiation?

Baptism and confirmation are what effect an enduring relation to the Church. This relation makes the believer fully capable of sharing in the Church's worship and mission.

307. How is the sacrament of baptism celebrated?

The celebration of baptism in the Latin rite culminates in the pouring of water over the forehead or the immersion of the person being baptized, accompanied by the words: "I baptize you in the name of the Father, and of the Son, and of the Holy Spirit."

308. What event in the Church's life of faith does baptism celebrate?

The baptismal celebration signifies a cleansing from sin and a rebirth into union with the risen Jesus. The symbolism of rebirth is more evident when baptism is celebrated by immersion as in the eastern rites. The person called to faith disappears under the cleansing waters and emerges a new creation in Christ.

309. What saving action of Christ does baptism accomplish?

Baptism effects incorporation into Christ's continuing body, the Church. Whatever of sin, original or personal, existed in a person's former life is simply wiped away by baptism. He is called to live in grace in the *mysterion* of the Church.

310. What is the "shape" of baptismal grace?

A baptized person forever belongs to the heavenly Father because of his everlasting love for his eternal Son, our savior. A baptized person becomes an adopted son or daughter of the Father. (See 1 Pt 1:3—4:11 for the most complete description of baptismal grace in the New Testament.)

311. Must actual tested and instructed faith in Jesus precede baptism?

The apostolic practice of baptizing whole households, presumably including infants, shows that actual tested and instructed faith in Jesus is not always necessary to become a member of the Church. Faith is a call, a gracious act on the part of God. Baptism is the "sealing" of that call by the Church.

Obviously, the Church would not discern faith's call in an unconvinced adult and would not baptize such a person. But one can discern faith's call when an infant has been born into a family of practicing Christians. It is their actual, adult faith which provides the evidence of God's graciousness to the infant. The Lord himself rebuked his disciples for presuming that children could not be the recipients of spiritual gifts (Mt 19:13-15).

312. Should infants be baptized indiscriminately?

Obviously not. If there is no reasonable guarantee of Christian upbringing, they should not be baptized. If the infant is in danger of death, the wishes of its parents should be respected. If these wishes are not known or cannot be reasonably presumed, one does what is best for the infant and baptizes it. In this last case, one presumes that the parents would wish the best for the infant if they understood the effects of baptism.

313. Could someone be an actual member of the Church without being baptized?

Yes, catechumens (persons under instruction) who die before baptism have always been recognized as actual Church members because of their desire for baptism. All the more is

"By baptism men are brought into the people of God"
(Vat. II: Ministry and Life of Priests, no. 5).

their actual membership recognized if the catechumen was martyred for the sake of the faith. Such Church membership is accomplished by a personal act of Christ responding to the catechumen's faith.

(Of course, if a catechumen is in danger of death, he should be baptized immediately. Perhaps the most famous example in church history of two catechumens who were baptized in prison before their martyrdom is the case of Vibia Perpetua, a noblewoman, and her slave Felicitas. They died in the arena of Carthage on March 7, 202.)

314. Who can administer baptism?

The normal minister of baptism is a Christian clergyman. But, in an emergency, anyone (Christian or not) can baptize as long as he intends to do what the Church does by this ritual. One pours or wipes natural water so that it runs on the skin of the forehead of the person (or the trunk of the body if the forehead cannot be reached). While doing so, one says: "I baptize you in the name of the Father, and of the Son, and of the Holy Spirit."

CONFIRMATION

315.   How is the sacrament of confirmation celebrated?

The celebration of confirmation in the Latin rite culminates in the imposition of the minister's hand while he anoints the recipient's forehead with blessed oil (chrism) and says: "Be sealed with the gift of the Holy Spirit."

316.   What event in the Church's life of faith does confirmation celebrate?

Strangely enough, the significance of confirmation is not at all settled in Church tradition. Confirmation, in some way, "finishes off" baptism. This "finishing-off" involves a communication of the gifts of the Holy Spirit for witnessing to Christ's Lordship. The Latin rite sees confirmation as a sacrament of Christian maturity which fits the recipient to live and defend his faith. The eastern rites see it as a sacrament which fits the recipient for profitable participation in the eucharist. (Interestingly, the Spanish Church follows the eastern rite tradition.)

317.   What is the "shape" of the grace of confirmation?

Just as the effect of confirmation is not totally clear, so the grace of confirmation is not clear. It would seem that a confirmed person's relation to the Father in Christ is "sealed" in the Holy Spirit—just as the union between Father and Son is forever unbroken in the Spirit.

318.   Who administers confirmation?

In the Latin rite, confirmation is usually administered by the bishop. As head of the local church, it seemed appropriate that he should complete a believer's Christian initiation. In the eastern rites, priests routinely administer confirmation at baptism. In the Latin rite, a priest may administer confirmation in cases of emergency. Likewise, the priest who instructs a convert may confirm him at the ceremony of reception.

319.   Who may be confirmed?

The tradition of the Church is unclear on who may be confirmed. In the Latin rite, confirmation is usually delayed until

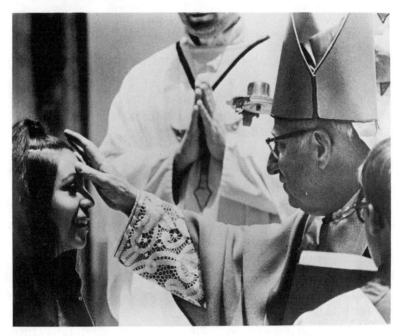

"Bound more intimately to the Church by the sacrament of confirmation, they are endowed by the Holy Spirit with special strength" (Vat. II: The Church, no. 11).

some time after first communion and preceded by a period of instruction. In the eastern rites, confirmation is administered to newly-baptized infants. In all rites, infants and children in danger of death are confirmed. (Since the Spanish-influenced churches follow the eastern tradition, children are often confirmed by the bishop before they make their first communion.)

Chapter 14

SACRAMENTS OF CRISIS

ANOINTING OF THE SICK

320. Why are the anointing of the sick and the reconciliation of penitents called sacraments of crisis?

They are called sacraments of crisis because each brings the saving action of Christ to bear on a situation which could break a person's spirit. Physical illness and moral failure can lead a person even to despair of the grace of God in Jesus Christ.

321. How does the Church celebrate the anointing of the sick?

The sacramental celebration in the Latin rite culminates in the anointing of the sick person with blessed oil on his forehead and his hands accompanied by the words: "Through this holy anointing may the Lord in his love and mercy help you with the grace of the Holy Spirit. Amen. May the Lord who frees you from sin save you and raise you up. Amen."

322. What event in the Church's life of faith does an anointing celebrate?

The anointing signifies a strengthening and a comforting of the sick person in spirit and body. The Church gives concrete assurance by the anointing that the care of Jesus for the afflicted continues.

323.   What saving action of Jesus is accomplished by an anointing?

The anointing effects a strengthening of the person's spirit to fight off the debilitating effects of illness or infirmity. This strength of spirit may also be an important factor in a person's physical recovery. The anointing also comforts the person's mind, especially if his conscience is not at ease. If the person needs forgiveness of sin and is unable to receive the sacrament of reconciliation (penance), the anointing forgives sin and removes the worries consequent upon sin.

324.   What is the "shape" of the grace of anointing?

The grace of anointing identifies the ill person with the obedient love of Christ who lived and died in utter trust that his heavenly Father would not abandon him. The same sort of obedient love relates the one anointed to the Father in Christ.

325.   Who may be anointed?

Anyone in a condition—be it physical or mental illness or mere age—which seriously impairs his health may be anointed. The judgment about impairment of health need not be a medical diagnosis. The person's own judgment about his state of health is sufficient grounds for anointing.

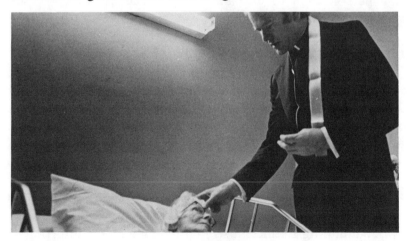

"By the sacred anointing of the sick and the prayer of the priests, the whole Church commends those who are ill to the suffering and glorified Lord" (Vat. II: The Church, no. 11).

326. When should a person be anointed?

A person should be anointed at the *onset* of the condition which seriously impairs his health. Anointing is not reserved only for the dying. It is not the "last sacrament." Holy communion is the last sacrament.

327. Can a person be anointed more than once?

The anointing of the sick may be routinely repeated every several months as the person's condition continues. It may be repeated immediately if the condition worsens.

328. May a dead person be anointed?

No, a dead person may not be anointed. If the fact of death is not fully established, a priest may anoint conditionally. Otherwise, the priest will simply pray for God's mercy on the deceased.

329. Who administers the anointing of the sick?

The letter of James (5:14) speaks of the "elders" of the Church as ministering to the sick. Thus, Church tradition has reserved the conferral of this sacrament to bishops and priests. There is some opinion that a deacon could be delegated to act in the name of the bishop or the parish priest in case of emergency.

330. Who should call the parish priest for an anointing?

Either the sick person himself or one who has care of him should call the priest at the *onset* of the condition. No false kindness to the ill person should prevent this information from being communicated. Priests do have tact in dealing with the sick and their sometimes irrational fears. What makes their task difficult is the irrational fear of those who are supposed to be caring for the sick.

331. What should be made ready for a sick call by a priest?

The Roman Ritual (no. 48) calls for a small table covered with a linen cloth in the sickroom. Other preparations are left to custom. In the United States, if holy communion is to be brought, it is customary to have a crucifix and two lighted blessed candles on the table.

RECONCILIATION OF PENITENTS

332. Is the sacrament of the reconciliation of penitents the same as the sacrament of penance or confession?

Yes, it is. As we shall discover, the sacrament has had a long history. Even the names for it have varied although "reconciliation" seems to bring out best what this sacrament effects. Catholic vocabulary has not quite settled in its usage as far as this sacrament is concerned.

333. How does the Church celebrate the reconciliation of penitents?

The celebration of the sacrament of reconciliation culminates in the penitent's confession of sin and expression of repentance followed by the confessor's words of forgiveness. Many formulas of absolution from sin have been used in the Latin rite.

The *Rite of Penance* (promulgated Dec. 2, 1973) prescribes the following: "God, the Father of mercies, through the death and resurrection of his Son has reconciled the world to himself and sent the Holy Spirit among us for the forgiveness of sins; through the ministry of the Church may God give you pardon and peace, and I absolve you from your sins in the name of the Father, and of the Son, and of the Holy Spirit. Amen."

334. What if actual confession of sin is impossible on the penitent's part?

Where sheer numbers or crowded conditions make actual confession impossible and a true spiritual urgency exists, a priest will lead the penitents in a general acknowledgment of sinfulness and repentance. Then he will grant general absolution. Where even this visible acknowledgment is impossible, as at a disaster-scene or when a person is unconscious, the priest will give general absolution conditionally.

In all such cases, the obligation of personal confession and expression of repentance still remains to be fulfilled. The *Rite of Penance* (no. 34) states that the recipient of general absolution, unless impeded by a just reason, may not receive general absolution again before he has made his individual confession.

335. **What event in the Church's life of faith does reconciliation celebrate?**

The obvious significance of the ritual is forgiveness of sin. But, beyond this, the tradition of the Church is clouded. Since sin can surely be forgiven to a truly repentant person prior to his reception of this sacrament, its effect is somewhat puzzling.

336. **But if sin can be forgiven by personal repentance, what does the sacrament of reconciliation effect over and above forgiveness?**

In order to understand the effect of the sacrament of reconciliation, a bit of Church history is in order:

a) Until the fifth century, the sacrament was administered after the pattern of an *excommunication* and could be received but *once*. No actual confession of sin was called for, since the sins for which reconciliation was sought were publicly known. The one seeking reconciliation was simply excluded, to an appropriate degree, from the celebration of the eucharist. When his penance, often of several years' duration, was completed, he was reconciled to the Church by the bishop and readmitted to full participation in the eucharist.

b) From the sixth century on, a way of administering the sacrament which originated in the Celtic monasteries became common. Celtic monks routinely confessed their private sins and faults to their abbot or his priest-delegate. The purpose of such confession was purity of conscience and growth in holiness. In such confessions, penance was purely private and no exclusion from the eucharist was involved. As the Celtic monks missionized northern Europe, this way of administering the sacrament became the instrument for Christianizing the barbarian tribes. Repeated confession and repeated penance inculcated the elements of moral behavior in peoples who scarcely knew the value of human life.

c) By the eleventh century, absolution was commonly granted even before the penance was performed. Exclusion from the eucharist was attached only to specific sins known as *crimina* and excommunication became a penalty rather than a part of the routine administration of the sacrament of reconciliation.

337. How does this bit of Church history clarify the effect of the sacrament of reconciliation?

It brings out *two* elements in the forgiveness of sin. It is these elements which the sacrament "shapes" out of the repentance of the sinner who may well already be forgiven. The elements are: *restored communion with the Church* and *ease of conscience.*

338. What saving action of Christ does the sacrament of reconciliation primarily accomplish: restored communion with the Church or ease of conscience?

Restored communion with the Church is the primary effect of the sacrament of reconciliation. The gospels always couple forgiveness with restored communion in discipleship (Mt 18:15ff; Jn 21:21-23). By historical accident, ease of conscience ("getting it off one's chest") has been presented as a selling-point for confession but this obscures what the sacrament of reconciliation effects.

339. Is there any practical consequence in knowing that restored communion with the Church is the effect of this sacrament?

Indeed, there is. It determines *what* sins must be confessed. Only those sins which put one out of communion with the Church *must* be confessed. All other sins may, but need not be, confessed.

340. What sins put one out of communion with the Church?

This sends us back to Church history. In the beginning, only sins which visibly harmed the "image" of the Church called for the reception of the sacrament of reconciliation, e.g., publicly known apostasy or murder or adultery, etc. As Christian moral sensitivity grew, it was seen that *any* sin which put the sinner totally at odds with the gospel was what really harmed the "image" of the Church.

Finally, the Council of Trent (1551, session 14) defined the matter: Any and all serious (mortal) sins must be confessed by *name* and *frequency.* Any other sins may be confessed as and how the penitent chooses.

341. What is the "shape" of the grace of the sacrament of reconciliation?

The grace of reconciliation restores the repentant sinner to unity of life with the Church. Fully in union with Christ, he can once again confidently call upon God as his Father knowing that he stands justified before him. If the penitent has no serious sin, his unity of life with the Church is strengthened, matured, and perfected by the sacrament.

342. Who administers the sacrament of reconciliation?

Because this sacrament has to do with restoration to Church life, only the bishop or a priest acting as the bishop's delegate may act as a confessor. Without the bishop's delegation, a priest may not act as a confessor except in emergency.

343. Who may receive the sacrament of reconciliation?

For ease of conscience, any repentant sinner for any sin may seek reconciliation by this sacrament.

344. Who must receive the sacrament of reconciliation?

A person in serious sin *must* seek reconciliation by this sacrament even if his repentance has already won forgiveness for his sin(s). He is at odds with the gospel as lived by the Church and his unity of life with the Church must be restored by the power of the risen Lord at work in the Church.

345. How often must the sacrament of reconciliation be received?

A person need never receive the sacrament of reconciliation if he has committed no serious sin. However, a person in *serious* sin must receive the sacrament of reconciliation:

a) Immediately, if he is in danger of death even from hazardous external circumstances.

b) By Church law (canon 916) if he wishes to receive holy communion.

c) By Church law (canon 989) once a year. (This is probably the calendar year. This obligation is not to be confused with the obligation to receive communion yearly during the Easter season. The two obligations may or may not be combined, depending upon circumstances.

GOING TO CONFESSION

346. Are there not many psychological difficulties in making a confession?

The Church tries to ease such difficulties by making confession as comfortable as possible. The penitent has perfect freedom in choosing any confessor he prefers. For those who prefer a formal confession, there is the opportunity provided by the public celebration of reconciliation where each penitent has a brief opportunity to confess to one of a number of confessors.

For those who prefer to remain completely anonymous and unrecognized, the classic confessional has a grating which conceals them from the confessor. For those who feel the need to make a more detailed confession and receive more personal advice, the confessional room provides an opportunity for a private interview with the confessor.

The priest helps the penitent make a good confession and gives him suitable counsel.

347. But it still is difficult to confess to another human being, isn't it?

The penitent should realize that the priest is a professional person and not likely to be shocked by anything he hears. Nor is the priest in the business of information-gathering or therapeutic probing. The confessor is there solely to exercise the reconciling ministry of Christ and he will be judged by God as to how well and tactfully he exercises it.

348. How does one go to confession?

If it is a group celebration of the sacrament, one simply follows the ceremony. When the opportunity for individual confession is offered, one goes to the confessor one has chosen and makes a brief and formal confession of one's sins. (If one feels the need at such a celebration for a more detailed and personal confession, it would seem wise to seek out a confessor in a confessional room.) An appendix to this lesson outlines the ceremony of individual confession.

PERSONAL REPENTANCE

349. How does one personally repent of sin?

Personal repentance involves two elements: contrition and amendment. Mindful of his sins and resolved to break with them, the sinner begs God's forgiveness through Christ's grace and resolves to better his life.

350. Does personal repentance win immediate forgiveness?

Yes, it does if the sinner's repentance is mature. Such mature or "perfect" contrition grows from regard for God's graciousness to humankind in Christ and a corresponding break with sin motivated by the sinner's ingratitude toward such sheer graciousness. Like the prodigal son (Lk 15:11-24), the sinner may begin with a consideration of his own miserable situation and then grow into an appreciation of what sort of response his acts have been to the goodness of his heavenly Father.

351. Does personal repentance based on self-regarding motives win immediate forgiveness?

No, it does not. Self-regarding motives, such as fear of hell, begin to make the sinner aware of his broken relation to God. But, by themselves, they produce only an immature or "imperfect" repentance. The sinner is not yet aiming at restoring the personal relation between himself and his heavenly Father in Christ. That relation, and that relation only, is grace.

352. Can immature contrition grow into mature contrition?

It can and it must if forgiveness is to be won. The sinner may seek after this growth by personal consideration of God's graciousness in Christ and corresponding prayer for the grace to deepen and mature his repentance.

353. Can one who has difficulties in achieving mature contrition receive the sacrament of reconciliation?

Indeed, he *should* receive the sacrament of reconciliation as devoutly as he can. It is Catholic doctrine that the sacrament of reconciliation *itself* is a means of making contrition mature (Council of Trent, session 11, 1551). But this maturing of contrition is not automatic. It depends upon the sinner's sincerity in seeking deliverance from what he himself knows to be immature repentance.

354. What aids does the Church provide to assist personal repentance?

In the liturgy, there are often services of repentance ("Penitential Celebrations"). Since the prayer of the risen Lord is joined with that of the participants, such services are most efficacious in winning forgiveness for sin. If, in addition, the sinner must seek restoration to the Church in the sacrament of reconciliation, such services dispose him to seek and receive the sacrament worthily.

ATONEMENT, INDULGENCES, AND PURGATORY

355. What does one do about the consequences of repented sin?

Such consequences must be *atoned for* to the best of one's capacities. We must undo the harm we have done to others and we must undo the harm we have done to our own character by appropriate acts of atonement.

356. What aids does the Church have for undoing the consequences of repented sin?

For the wrongs which are beyond our control or capacities to undo, the Church begs God for an *indulgence*. Relying on the merits of Christ, which can undo all wrong, the Church begs God to accept them in place of the sinner's own atonement. Indulgences are attached to specific prayers and good works.

357. What must one do to gain an indulgence?

Usually, indulgences call for the reception of the sacrament of reconciliation, holy communion, prayer for the intentions of the Pope, and the performance of the prescribed prayer or good work. Some indulgences are plenary, some are partial, i.e., the Church begs God to undo all or some of the consequences of repented sin. Indulgences are not automatic. They depend upon the sincerity of the sinner's personal repentance and his personal determination to atone for the consequences of his sins.

358. What about someone who dies truly repentant but who has not atoned for all his sins?

Such a departed soul needs *purgation* in order to experience the blessed communion of Son and Father in the Holy Spirit. This is the Catholic doctrine of purgatory solemnly defined at the second council of Lyons (1274). The roots of the doctrine lie in the constant practice of the Church of praying for the departed. The practice was taken over, almost casually, from late Judaism (2 Mac 12:39-45) and deepened by the Church's awareness of Jesus' many remarks about the thoroughness of God's judgment.

359. What is purgatory?

Aside from the existence of such a state, the tradition of the Church is not consistent. Perhaps the safest thing to say is that purgatory is a state in which a deceased person works free of the consequences of sin. What he must learn are the lessons of Christian discipleship he failed to learn during life. But by what means he learns and practices them, we do not know.

360. How does one pray for the departed?

Surely, having Masses celebrated for the departed is a most efficacious prayer for them. Personal prayer for the departed can take two forms: (a) begging God's indulgence for them; (b) doing good works in their memory. Any indulgenced prayer or work can be applied to a departed person. Surely, too, any good work done in memory of the departed, especially if it is one he failed to do, is a most acceptable and Christian prayer for him.

APPENDIX: INDIVIDUAL CONFESSION

No preparatory ceremony is involved in an individual confession. The penitent prepares himself either at home or in the church before he enters the confessional or confessional room. He begins with prayer to the Holy Spirit for enlightenment. Next he examines his conscience and arranges in his memory the sins (and their frequency) he needs or wishes to confess. Then he makes a private act of repentance.

A suggested formula: "O God, my Father, I am truly sorry for my sins. I acknowledge that I deserve your just judgment but I beg your mercy. Above all, I am sorry because I have offended your goodness and graciousness to me in Christ. I am resolved to avoid sin and what leads to sin."

Now the penitent is ready to make his confession. Some device, usually a light, indicates whether a confessor is available and whether a penitent is already in the confessional or confessional room. If the priest is occupied with a penitent, then the next penitent simply waits his turn being careful not to stand too close to the entrance lest he overhear anything.

If the penitent is making his confession in the classic confessional, he kneels before the grating and *waits* until the confessor opens the slide. If the penitent is making his confession in a confessional room, the option of kneeling before the grating or going around it and being seated facing the confessor is for the penitent to make.

The confessor greets the penitent and invites him to make the sign of the cross. Next the confessor says a brief prayer that the penitent may have confidence in God's forgiving mercy. Then, at the option of priest or penitent, a brief reading from the Bible may follow. (It would seem prudent to omit this reading if the penitent's confession is what is in the forefront of his mind. The penitent himself could request this in order to get his confession over with.)

Now the penitent begins his confession.

The confessor may help the penitent to better express and understand what he is confessing. The confessor may also give him suitable counsel adapted to his circumstances. Then the confessor proposes an appropriate act of penance which the penitent accepts as a means of making satisfaction for his sins and amending his life.

The priest asks the penitent to express his sorrow either in his own words or by leading him in a prayer of contrition. Finally, the confessor extends his hand(s) over the penitent's head and pronounces the words of absolution. The priest then concludes with a brief prayer of praise: "Give thanks to the Lord, for he is good." The penitent responds: "His mercy endures forever."

A moment of thanksgiving on the penitent's part would seem most appropriate if the sacrament has been administered in church. So, too, if prayers have been assigned as his penance, if would be most appropriate to say them at this time.

Chapter 15

SACRAMENTS OF VOCATION

HOLY ORDERS

361. Why are holy orders and matrimony called sacraments of vocation?

Holy orders and matrimony are called sacraments of vocation because each graces a state of life. Holy orders graces a life of ministry in the Church. Matrimony graces a life of love and fidelity between husband and wife.

362. How does the Church celebrate an ordination?

The sacramental celebration of holy orders culminates in the imposition of the minister's hands upon the head of the candidate, accompanied by an invocation of the Holy Spirit to grace the recipient for service to the Church. The invocation varies depending upon what grade of service is being communicated: deacon, priest, or bishop.

363. What event in the Church's life of faith does an ordination celebrate?

The ordination ritual signifies a choosing-out of the recipient for a life of ministry to the Church. The very spirit of Christ, who came to serve, is to be the spirit of the ordinand's life.

364. What saving action of Christ is accomplished by ordination?

The sacrament of ordination effects a special, public gift of ministry in the recipient, over and above the gift of ministering which is common to the whole Church. The one ordained becomes a public person available always for the Church's needs. He is given the evangelical authority to serve as Christ served.

365. What is the "shape" of the grace of ordination?

The grace of ordination identifies the one ordained with Christ, the servant-savior. Deacons, priests, and bishops work out their salvation by making that identity real in their lives and work. That is their special relation in Christ to the heavenly Father.

366. Who administers the sacrament of holy orders?

Church tradition in all the rites reserves the conferring of ordination to a bishop. The choosing-out of candidates for the service of the Church is the task and privilege of one whose total life is one of care for the Church.

367. Who may be ordained?

In all rites of the Church, only males have ever been ordained. Between the fourth and eleventh centuries, in the Latin rite, the custom or ordaining only celibate males became law. In the eastern rites, married men may be ordained deacons and priests, but bishops must be celibate. In all rites, clergymen may not marry after ordination. An exception to Latin rite celibacy is made in the case of mature married men who wish to serve the Church as non-salaried deacons.

368. Will the rule of celibacy ever be relaxed in the Latin rite?

As far as the routine ordination of married men to all grades of orders is concerned, no relaxation of the discipline of celibacy is foreseeable. Celibacy has service-value because the unmarried clergyman is free from the overriding responsibilities of wife and family (see 1 Cor 7:32-33). Celibacy also has a sign-value in that the unmarried clergyman is free to exemplify the overriding values of the kingdom of heaven to a world which is passing away (see Mt 19:12).

369.   Doesn't the Bible say that clergymen should be married?

What the Bible does say is that a presiding elder (bishop?) should not have been married more than once (1 Tm 3:2). What this means is that Church leaders, if they are widowers, should set a decent example of respect for their departed wives and not remarry. The author of the letter to Timothy is concerned that the infant churches have a good reputation among the pagans. His rule is a minimum requirement for respectability. For St. Paul's example and preference, see the seventh chapter of First Corinthians.

370.   Will women ever be ordained?

There does not seem to be any theoretical objection to the ordination of women. In Christ, there is no distinction between male and female (Gal 3:28). Perhaps the constant practice of ordaining only males has just been the most expedient thing to do in male-dominated societies. Or, perhaps, it has a genuine sanction in Church tradition.

If there is such a sanction, it cannot rest upon the supposition that there is something about women which makes them unfit for ordination. Rather, it would have to rest upon some essential distinction in the roles of service to the Church proper to men and women.

371.   What course of studies does a Catholic clergyman take?

A Catholic clergyman is usually a college graduate who has done four years of postgraduate theological study and pastoral internship.

"Those of the faithful who are consecrated in holy orders are appointed to feed the Church in Christ's name with the Word and the grace of God" (Vat. II: The Church, no. 11).

372. May a Catholic clergyman resign his ministry?

Reluctantly, a clergyman's resignation from the ministry will be accepted and dispensation from celibacy will be granted. Without such a dispensation, a clergyman's marriage is invalid (canon 1087); he is automatically deprived of office (canon 194 §1, 3°) and automatically suspended from functioning as a clergyman (canon 1394).

The resignation is, by its nature, perpetual and the clergyman may never licitly function again unless someone is in danger of death and no other clergyman is available. Included in the dispensation are instructions to the clergyman's ecclesiastical superiors making sure that he has the necessary aids to begin his new life.

MATRIMONY

373. How does the Church celebrate a marriage?

The visible ritual of matrimony is the mutual consent exchanged between bride and groom to be husband and wife. It is usually in the form of a marriage vow spoken by each to the other. The Roman Ritual suggests: "I, N., take you, N., to be my husband/wife. I promise to be true to you in good times and in bad, in sickness and in health. I will love you and honor you all the days of my life."

374. What event in the Church's life of faith does matrimony celebrate?

Strangely enough, what the marriage vow *says* has no particular sacramental significance. The marriage vow refers to the institution of marriage and, thus, could be spoken by a couple of any or no religious faith. Thus, there must be something about the vowing of Christian spouses, some added dimension, which makes their unity-in-life a sacrament.

375. What does the Bible teach about the institution of marriage?

The whole Bible presupposes that marriage, in itself, is naturally honorable and holy. God's creation of man and woman is his supreme achievement (Gn 2:18-24). The prophets see marriage as a *covenant* like unto and an image of the covenant between Yahweh and Israel. For instance, the first three chapters of Hosea are the most heart-rending picture of violated covenant-love in the whole Bible (see also Micah 2:10-16). In the love-poetry of the Song of Songs, marriage and covenant-love simply merge.

The New Testament adopts and deepens these Old Testament themes by comparing the love of husband and wife to the love between Christ and the Church. The climactic passage is the fifth chapter of Ephesians.

376.   Is marriage a covenant?

Yes, it is. The marriage vow expresses the unity-in-life of husband and wife. This is what provides the enduring foundation for a family in which children can be lovingly begotten and raised. (See Tobit, 8:5-8, for a beautiful Old Testament prayer of a newly-married couple.) Such a pledge can scarcely be reduced to a contract with performance clauses and penalties.

The marriage vow is a pledge of lifelong fidelity. Someone wisely observed: "Contracts can be broken; covenants can only be violated." Perhaps the experience of both those who have succeeded and those who have failed at marriage is the best witness that the marriage vow is a covenanting in love, not a contracting in mutual rights and duties.

377.   What added dimension is there to the unity-in-life of Christian spouses which makes their marriage a sacrament?

The unity-in-life of those who marry "in the Lord" is created by the very power of the risen savior. St. Paul sees a strict parallel between marriage "in the Lord" and the unity-of-life between Christ and the Church (Eph 5:20ff). A Christian family is the place where the hidden power of Jesus to transform human relations becomes visible in the world. The only other place like it is the Church.

378.   What saving action of Christ is accomplished by the sacrament of matrimony?

"Married Christians, in virtue of the sacrament of matrimony, signify and share in the mystery of that unity and fruitful love which exists between Christ and his Church; they help each other to attain to holiness in their married life and in the rearing and education of their children; and they have their own special gift among the people of God" (Roman Ritual: Rite of Marriage, no. 1). The important words are "unity" and "fruitful love" like to that which exists at the heart of the Church itself.

379.   What is the "shape" of the grace of matrimony?

What the sacrament of matrimony especially graces is the mutual surrender and self-forgetfulness which marriage naturally demands of husband and wife. Just as the risen savior lives for his Church and the Church, in turn, lives for its Lord, so husband and wife work out their salvation by making this same kind of mutually faithful covenant-love apparent in their family.

380.   Who administers the sacrament of matrimony?

The bride and groom administer the sacrament of matrimony to each other. However, both society and the Church have instituted legal requirements which must be met for a marriage to be valid.

"Christian spouses, in virtue of the sacrament of matrimony, signify and partake of that unity and fruitful love which exists between Christ and his Church" (Vat. II: The Church, no. 11).

CATHOLIC LAW ON MARRIAGE

381. What are the Catholic Church's legal requirements for marriage?

If, and *only if,* one or both parties to a marriage are Catholic, the marriage must be celebrated in the presence of a Catholic clergyman (bishop, priest, or deacon) and two witnesses. (For some exceptions, see questions 199, 204-205.) The original purpose of this law was to prevent clandestine marriages, i.e., marriages which were absolutely unverifiable except on the word of the parties themselves.

Even though clandestine marriages are almost impossible today, the law was still seen as a good one. It expresses the belief of the Church that marriage is not a private affair between the couple but a public avowal before the believing community of their sacred commitment to each other.

382. Are non-Catholic marriages recognized as valid and sacramental by the Catholic Church?

They are. The Catholic Church recognizes marriages between non-Catholics as valid and, if both parties are baptized, as sacramental as long as the proper legal requirements have been fulfilled.

383. Suppose a Catholic did not get married before a Catholic clergyman. What must he do if he wishes to sacramentalize his marriage?

He must renew and ratify his marriage vows before a Catholic clergyman and two witnesses. Catholics speak of this as having a marriage "blessed." The correct legal term is *convalidation.* All the Church's legal requirements must be met for a marriage to be convalidated. The ceremony is usually performed privately to spare the couple any embarrassment.

384. Who may be married?

Since marriage is a natural right, any couple of sufficient maturity can marry if there is no impediment to their union. However, both society and the Church have an interest in seeing that this natural right is exercised wisely. An appendix to this lesson outlines the present Church law on marriage and the reasons for its main features. This law is followed even when a marriage is being convalidated.

MIXED MARRIAGES

385. Will the Catholic Church ever change in its opposition to mixed marriages?

All religious bodies are concerned about interfaith or interdenominational marriages. Unity-in-life between partners who sincerely maintain different religious values is extremely difficult to maintain, especially when it comes to the religious education of their children. Yet, marriage is a *natural* right. So the various faiths do their best to minimize the difficulties facing an interfaith or interdenominational couple.

386. What sort of prenuptial agreement does a Catholic have to make in order to marry a non-Catholic?

The Catholic party must reaffirm his or her faith as a Catholic Christian and promise to undertake the Church law obligation to see to his or her children's Catholic baptism and upbringing as far as possible.

387. What sort of prenuptial agreement does a non-Catholic have to make in order to marry a Catholic?

The non-Catholic does not have to make any formal agreement. He or she, however, must be informed of the Catholic party's agreement. The priest arranging for the marriage must so testify.

388. Isn't this prenuptial agreement unfair to the non-Catholic?

A distinction must be made in order to answer this question. One part of the agreement involves the *natural* obligation of the Catholic party to follow his or her conscience. Surely a non-Catholic ought not enter into marriage intending to violate another's rights in such a crucial matter. The other part of the agreement involves a *Church law* obligation on the part of the Catholic party concerning the religious upbringing of the children. The fairness of this, in all cases, may be open to some question.

389. Could the Catholic Church dispense from the promise that the children of a mixed marriage be given a Catholic upbringing?

Dispensing from this requirement poses a neat dilemma between law (canon 1125) and fact. The law embodies the Catholic Church's conviction that it is fully Christ's Church and, thus, tries to safeguard the salvation of the children. But the fact is that a poor Catholic upbringing might put the child in more peril than a good upbringing in another Christian denomination, or, perhaps, even in another religion.

Some theologians argue that this requirement ought to be routinely dispensed with when the Catholic is only nominally religious and his or her future spouse is a devout Christian of another denomination.

390. Wouldn't giving such a dispensation be the most sensible solution where the parties to a mixed marriage have not agreed on the religious upbringing of their children?

It all depends on what is meant by "not agreed." If there is a real, reasoned *disagreement* between the parties, perhaps the most sensible solution might be a dispensation in order to assure some sort of religious upbringing for the children. But if there has simply been no discussion of the reality of their religious differences between the parties, then a dispensation seems out of order.

What needs to be determined is the *reason* for the avoidance of discussion of what is a most important factor in the marriage. The most frustrating dilemma a priest can be put into is the situation where the Catholic party to a mixed marriage has avoided all discussion of religion in the vague hope that "Father will take care of it."

APPENDIX: PREPARING FOR A CATHOLIC MARRIAGE

The legal formalities for a Catholic marriage can be lengthy. It is wise to arrange for a marriage at least six weeks ahead, or even sooner, if complications are foreseen. If both parties are Catholic, the priest to contact is the pastor of the bride. If only one party is Catholic, the priest to contact is his or her pastor. Even if the wedding will not take place in this pastor's church, his permission is needed for the marriage to proceed. Likewise, the parties should be sure that the church is free for the ceremony. Otherwise, much embarrassment may occur and invitations have to be reprinted.

1) *Documents:* Catholic parties must present a newly-issued copy of their baptismal certificate dated within six months of the wedding. They must also present any copy of their first communion and confirmation certificate. (The newly-issued baptismal certificate is part of the proof of "freedom of state." If a Catholic has previously been married in the Church, a note of that fact appears on his baptismal certificate.)

A non-Catholic must present any record of his baptism. If he or she has never been baptized, no documents need be presented.

2) *Pastoral Instructions:* A Catholic couple are given at least one pastoral instruction on marriage. The priest himself may give the instruction or he may recommend attendance at a pre-Cana conference at which various experts speak on the different aspects of marriage.

If one party to the marriage is a non-Catholic, some instruction in the Catholic religion is given. The purpose of the instruction(s) is not to convert the non-Catholic but to make sure that no basic religious misunderstandings will crop up in the marriage. Most diocesan statutes speak of six instructions but allow the priest to interpret the statute to fit the situation.

3) *Affidavits:* Each party is questioned separately about identity, religious background, understanding of marriage, and "freedom of state." The point of the affidavit is to make sure that the parties are truly free to marry: free from any impediment (including a previous spouse) and free in their decision to take each other as man and wife. If any dispensation or a declaration of nullity of a previous marriage is needed, the marriage cannot proceed until it is granted.

Each party also selects a character witness to fill out a similar affidavit as testimony to his or her "freedom of state." A parent, close relative, or close friend is usually chosen. This affidavit can be sent to the character witness who then takes it to the nearest priest to fill out.

"Sealed by mutual faithfulness and hallowed above all by Christ's sacrament, this love of the spouses remains steadfastly true in body and in mind, in bright days or dark" (Vat. II: The Church in the Modern World, no. 49).

4) Ceremony: Priests are willing to agree to specific requests for music or special ceremonies if they are in good taste and appropriate to a church wedding. Fees should also be discussed as the ceremony is being planned lest there be any misunderstandings to mar the beauty of the wedding. Finally, the couple should not forget to obtain their *civil license.* A rehearsal is usually held a day or so before the ceremony.

Chapter 16

DIVORCE AND REMARRIAGE

JESUS' TEACHING ON DIVORCE

391. Does the Catholic Church believe in divorce and remarriage?

No, it does not. The reasons for this belief are found in the teachings of Jesus himself (Mt 19:1-12; Mk 10:1-12; Lk 16:18).

392. What does Jesus teach about divorce?

The most detailed account is found in Matthew's gospel (19:1-12). Some Pharisees approach Jesus and challenge him with a knotty case in Jewish law: Can a man divorce his wife for just any reason whatsoever? Jesus undercuts their basic assumption that marriage is just a contract by referring them to Genesis (2:24), the very founding-book of Judaism. "In the beginning" God himself made man and wife one. Therefore, no human authority can dissolve their unity-in-life.

The Pharisees are shocked. Why, then, did the law of Moses command a bill of divorce in such cases (Dt 24:1)? Jesus replies that not even Moses could do much to teach them the ideal recorded in their own founding-book. Jesus is saying that the Mosaic law simply tried to protect the woman from being thrown out on the street in a lamentable situation. Jesus then concludes with a flat statement that one who divorces and remarries is guilty of adultery.

393. How do Jesus' disciples react to his flat prohibition of divorce and remarriage?

They remark to him that such an ideal of marriage is not humanly possible. But, even under pressure from his own disciples, Jesus does not modify his teaching. He merely remarks that chastity, unless forced on someone, is also humanly impossible. Jesus is saying that lasting faithfulness to any ideal is always a particular work of God's grace and cannot be judged in human terms.

394. Doesn't Jesus make an exception to his prohibition of divorce?

Only in Matthew (19:9) *porneia* is mentioned as a separate case. *Porneia* means shamelessness or wantonness. The exact case is not possible to determine from the casual reference in Matthew. (If shameless or wanton unfaithfulness is meant, it could be that Jesus is saying that it would be grounds for separation. Or it could be that Jesus is saying that shameless or wanton promiscuity makes it impossible for a person to enter into marriage in the first place.)

395. Could it be that Jesus is proposing an ideal of marriage which, in fact, need not always be lived up to?

One could, perhaps, argue that the dissolution of a less-than-ideal marriage might be the less-than-ideal solution to an otherwise insoluble problem. But, equally, Jesus is saying that a couple who enter into marriage with the possibility of divorce in mind have already closed themselves off from ever achieving the divinely-graced faithfulness proper to marriage. Even more, Jesus is teaching that a society with a divorce-mentality is itself wrongly oriented. In the case of marriage, to aim at less than the ideal is to miss the whole target.

396. But if Jesus' teaching on marriage proposes an ideal, could it be that his prohibition of divorce and remarriage is also an ideal which cannot always be lived up to?

Jesus' teaching that one who remarries commits adultery stresses that his prohibition of divorce and remarriage is absolute. What Jesus wants to do is to root out completely the divorce-mentality itself. Those who would be his disciples can have nothing to do with such a mentality. Marriage, for them, is absolutely indissoluble.

DISSOLUTION AND ANNULMENT OF MARRIAGE

397. Can the Church dissolve a sacramental marriage?

No, the Church would go against the gospels in presuming to dissolve a sacramental marriage. Note carefully that any marriage between baptized persons (not just between Catholics) is presumed to be sacramental unless proved otherwise.

398. Can the Church dissolve a non-sacramental marriage?

No, except for one special case, the Church has no authority to dissolve a non-sacramental marriage. Nor, according to Jesus' teaching, do the parties themselves, or any human authority, have such power.

399. What is the special case in which the Church can dissolve a non-sacramental marriage?

This special case is outlined in the New Testament (1 Cor 7:12-16). Suppose that a non-sacramental marriage is a real obstacle to someone's becoming a member of the Church. On the principle that baptism is a rebirth into a completely new life, the Church will break the previous bond "in favor of the faith." The person is free from the moment of baptism to remarry "in the Lord." Depending on the circumstances, this is called the "Pauline privilege" or a "privilege of the faith" case.

400. Are there such things as Church annulments of marriages?

Yes, there are. Distinguish carefully between dissolution of a marriage and annulment of a marriage. An annulment is a declaration by a Church court that a marriage was null and void *to begin with*. Grounds for annulment must always be proved and the process can be lengthy.

401. What are the grounds for a Church annulment?

The general grounds for annulment are: (a) lack of intention to marry; (b) physical or psychological incapacity to marry; (c) undue force or pressure to marry; (d) fraudulent representations or promises connected with marrying, and; (e) unfulfilled conditions attached to marrying.

402.   Could the grounds for annulment be widened from the ones which have been mentioned?

Yes, the grounds for annulment could be widened. In our divorce-prone and post-Christian society, the Church could even make it a presumption in law that a marriage is null and void unless it is proved otherwise. But that would be bad law. Good law must presume right intentions unless the opposite can be proved.

403.   If the grounds for annulment should not be widened, what other stand on the part of Church law would be appropriate in our post-Christian and divorce-prone society?

Perhaps the wisest legal safeguard of the indissolubility of a sacramental marriage would be the institution of additional *impediments* to a Church wedding. Another solution might be for the bishop to exercise his right to delay a marriage (canon 1077 §1). Some Catholic dioceses have instituted rigorous preliminaries to marriages between young persons, especially if pregnancy is involved.

404.   Can nothing be done for a Catholic who has failed to prove (or cannot prove) the grounds for a Church annulment but, in conscience, knows that they exist?

Nothing judicial can be done. A Church court, like any court, has to go by the evidence. What one has here is a case of conscience which has to be settled extra-judicially.

405.   What is a case of conscience?

In general, a case of conscience is a situation in which someone, dispassionately and objectively, judges the rightness or wrongness of his behavior. As applied to marriage, a case of conscience is a person's own examination of the circumstances of his marrying as to their rightness or wrongness.

406.   But wouldn't some priest have to declare on the merits of such a case of conscience?

No, that would make the priest a sort of mini-court rendering a judgment. Rather, a priest would act in his pastoral capacity as a confessor or spiritual director helping the party examine his own conscience without self-deception or rationalization about the circumstances of his marrying.

PROBLEMS OF REMARRIAGE

407. Are there any church penalties for getting a civil divorce and remarrying?

No, there are not. But most diocesan statutes insist that Church permission be obtained for getting a civil divorce. This is to insure that a Catholic does not act rashly or, depending on motives, even sinfully in separating from his spouse. Such permission implies *no* permission to remarry.

408. What can be done for remarried Catholics who cannot separate because of the children or other pressing reasons?

The case of a second marriage in which there is an obligation to maintain family life poses a real moral dilemma. There is something *wrong* about the marriage and the evangelical authority of the Church cannot right it. Yet, in conscience, the parties have to live with and live out their marriage as it actually exists. Catholic parties to such a marriage are prevented from routine reception of the sacraments. This is a matter of Church order enacted to prevent scandal to the whole body of the faithful.

Yet, Church attendance, prayer, Christian living, and the religious education of their children are surely not ruled out for persons in such a situation. The prayer of the risen Lord in and for his Church does not exclude their very special needs. And, surely, that prayer wins grace for those who are doing their best to live rightly in such a moral dilemma. Thus, no one may judge that such a couple is living in sin.

Chapter 17

MARY — MOTHER AND DISCIPLE

MARY IN THE GOSPELS

409. Why do Catholics pay such great honor to Mary, the mother of Jesus?

Catholics reverence the person of Mary for two interconnected reasons: (a) because she was chosen to be the mother according to the flesh of the eternal Son of God; (b) because she was the perfect disciple of her son.

410. Is it really true to say that Mary is the mother of God?

Yes, Mary is truly the mother of God according to the flesh. Mothers bear *persons,* not just bodies. And the person whom Mary bore is truly the eternal Son of God, one in divinity with the Father (Council of Ephesus, 431).

411. But is Mary's mere physical maternity enough to explain the honor given to her by Catholics?

No, it is not. As the gospels portray Mary, her role in salvation does not end with the birth of Jesus. St. John's gospel, for instance, puts Mary at both the beginning and the ending of Jesus' public life (Jn 2:1-12; 19:25-27). In both scenes, Mary is presented as the woman of true discernment, with utter faith in her son's mission. In turn, her son reverences her with the utmost respect. There is something about the very *person* of Mary which enables her to enter uniquely into the life and task of her son.

412. Just who is Mary, the mother of Jesus?

The first two chapters of St. Luke's gospel best portray the person of Mary. These chapters are filled with delicate allusions to all the great women of Israel who played crucial roles in the history of salvation. In this framework, Luke gives his account of Jesus' conception and birth. Mary is proclaimed blessed, not just because she is to be the Messiah's mother, but because she herself is the perfection of all the women who believed in Yahweh's saving actions. It is Mary's *faith* which merits her role in the final accomplishment of humankind's salvation.

413. But doesn't Jesus reject Mary at one place in the gospels?

In the incident of the "true kinsman" (Mt 12:46-50), Jesus points out that faith, not blood, determines who are true kin to him. There is no implication that his blood-relations could not also become his disciples and, thus, his true kin. In a later incident (Lk 11:27-28), Jesus accepts a compliment paid to his mother and simply adds the remark about who are his true kin. Perhaps Jesus' remark: "Rather, blest are they who hear the word of God and keep it" is his own added compliment to his mother.

MARY'S UNSURPASSED HOLINESS

414. What has the Catholic Church discerned from the gospel-picture of Mary, the mother of Jesus?

The tradition of the Church has discerned in Mary a work of unsurpassed holiness. The tradition grew rather casually out of ordinary piety. In fact, some theologians contested the holiness which the ordinary faithful attributed to Mary. They felt it could put Mary completely outside the need for salvation.

415. Did Mary need Christ's saving grace?

Yes, she did. Her origin, like ours, was a human origin and needed redemption. Her holiness, like ours, is the work of Jesus' sacrifice and victory. Her unsurpassed holiness is the supreme achievement of the grace of God in Christ. Thus, Mary is the model of what the Church aspires to become.

416.   Have all the aspects of Mary's unsurpassed holiness been determined in Church doctrine?

No, the exploration of Mary's holiness still goes on. Two aspects of her holiness, however, have become formally defined doctrine. Interestingly enough, these two doctrinal definitions are also the only two uses of direct papal infallibility.

417.   What two aspects of Mary's holiness have become defined doctrine?

The two aspects of Mary's holiness which have become defined doctrine are her immaculate conception (Pius IX, 1854) and her bodily assumption into eternal life (Pius XII, 1950).

418.   What is the doctrine of Mary's immaculate conception?

This doctrine states that Mary's salvation by Christ's grace was accomplished at the very moment of her human origin. The doctrine discerns *why* she was perfect and unfaltering in her faith. Sinless in origin, she grew uninterruptedly in her relation to God and so merited to become both mother and perfect disciple of Jesus.

National Shrine of the Immaculate Conception, Washington, D.C.

419. What is the doctrine of Mary's bodily assumption into eternal life?

This doctrine states the *outcome* of Mary's unsurpassed holiness. Perfect in faith and grace at every stage of her life, she merited the fullness of eternal life at her life's end. The victory of her son over death is already complete in her.

MARY AND THE CHURCH

420. What aspects of Mary's holiness are still under study?

There are two lines of study going on. One concentrates on Mary's personal prerogatives as mother and perfect disciple of Jesus. The other line of study concentrates on Mary as the model or example of what the Church aspires to become. In fact, the two lines of study are converging.

421. What does this convergence of studies of Mary and studies of the Church mean?

These convergent studies refine and deepen the insights of ordinary piety. For instance, ordinary piety has always discerned that Mary, somehow, is the mother of all believers. But deeper reflection upon the fact that the Church is Christ's very continuing body suggests that Mary's motherhood of all believers is more than just a sort of natural care and concern for those who believe in her son. Her motherhood of believers is rooted in her personal acceptance and understanding of her very motherhood of Jesus himself.

422. Can you give another example of the convergence of studies of Mary and studies of the Church?

Ordinary piety has always called upon Christians to imitate Mary as well as to reverence her. But how? If one studies Mary as a model of what the Church aspires to become, one sees that her persevering and courageous faith provide inspiration for any Christian as he attempts to live out the gospel. It is Mary's discipleship which is our model.

423. How does ordinary piety express Mary's role in our salvation?

Ordinary piety weaves together the two threads of Mary's maternal care of Christians and the value of imitation of Mary.

For instance, the rosary combines prayer to Mary with pondering in our hearts, like Mary, on the chief gospel-events. So, too, scapulars and medals are worn to honor her as mother of believers and as reminders to us of our Christian commitment. One simple ancient prayer sums it all up: "Pray for us, O holy mother of God, that we may be made worthy of the promises of Christ."

SAINTS

424. What about Catholic veneration of the saints?

Just as Mary's relation is always to Christ and the Church, so the saints are not some sort of sub-mediators between humankind and God, our Father. Only Christ mediates between man and God (1 Tm 2:5-6). The saints are intercessors with Christ and examples of Christ's grace for our imitation. Products of the Church, they pray for its fulfillment and exemplify a multitude of ways according to which the gospel can be lived.

425. How is a person named a saint?

Many saints, of course, are known but to God. Saints are named by canonization, i.e., on the day of their naming, they are mentioned in the canon or eucharistic prayer. Ancient saints were named by popular acclaim. Gradually, the process was taken over by a bishop's court and, since the seventeenth century, by a papal court. The formal process consists in a searching inquiry into the person's life and evidence of miracles due to his intercession with Christ for the Church.

426. Is a person ever "un-named" a saint?

Periodically, the list of the saints is reviewed for its accuracy. In the last review, for instance, the name of St. Christopher was removed because it did not name a person. The entry on the list commemorated an unknown, holy Christian, not someone specifically named "Christopher."

427. What determines a saint's feast day?

Usually, a saint's feast day marks the date of his death, i.e., his heavenly birthday. Sometimes, though, it marks some great event in his life or some miracle worked by his intercession.

428. What determines what a saint is patron of?

Sometimes, some personal characteristic of the saint determines what he is patron of, e.g., St. Francis of Assisi's love for animals has made him patron saint of animals. Sometimes, the reason is a bit more fanciful. St. Jude Thaddeus, the apostle, is patron saint of the impossible because of the similarity of his name to the betrayer, Judas. People felt that the mix-up of names would prevent St. Jude from getting many prayers. So, he would do his utmost no matter how difficult the request. The Church has a sense of humor and, one suspects, the saints do, too.

429. How did the saints become saints?

There is no particular secret to Christian holiness. The saints became saints by becoming disciples of Jesus in the Church.

430. How does one become a disciple of Jesus today?

One becomes a disciple today by experiencing the gospel as lived and proclaimed by the Church. Hearing the gosepl preached and meditating on its personal implications is the indispensable condition for Christian holiness. As aids to our spiritual discernment, the Church presents to us Mary and the multitude of the saints. Some saints have even written accounts of their progress in holiness. These the Church recognizes as its "doctors" or teachers.

RELIGIOUS ORDERS

431. Has the Church instituted any means for achieving Christian holiness?

The Church itself is the school of Christian holiness and all its members, from least to greatest, learn in it. However, means have grown up in the Church whereby communities of Christian men and women seek after holiness by following a specific rule of life. These are the religious orders.

432. How do religious orders pursue Christian holiness?

There have been a bewildering variety of religious orders in the Church. Two elements, however, are common to all: (a) a rule of life; (b) vows or promises ᴖf obedience, celibacy, and poverty. The rule determines the community's understanding of the gospel and the vows specify the particular form of Christian asceticism the community has chosen to follow.

433. What is the relation of a religious order to the Church?

Religious orders are voluntary associations of Christians within the Church. Once their rule of life is approved by the Church, their internal affairs are regulated by their own authorities. Whatever work they choose to undertake must be acceptable to the appropriate Church authority. If some or all of their members are priests, their ministry is under the bishop's control.

434. How does a person become a member of a religious order?

One who is attracted to a religious order makes contact with the authorities of the order. A visit and interview is arranged so each can get acquainted with the other. If accepted, a candidate then enters a preparatory program in which he lives the life of the community, is given an education appropriate to its work, and learns its spirit and customs. During this period, either the candidate or the order can terminate their connection. At its conclusion, the candidate petitions for admission and, if accepted, is admitted to membership and vows.

Chapter 18

CHRISTIAN HOLINESS

HOLINESS AND GRACE

435. What is Christian holiness?

Holiness, in general, is being and doing that which pleases God. Since the gospels clearly show that Jesus' loving obedience to the Father is what pleases God, it follows that Christian holiness is something quite concrete. To the extent that a Christian shares in Christ's own loving obedience to the Father, he is holy.

436. How does a Christian share in Christ's loving obedience to the Father?

He shares in it by grace. But neither this way of putting the question nor the answer does justice to what Christian holiness really is. The question makes it sound as if a Christian, somehow, has to achieve a holy relation to God instead of being sanctified by his very faith in Jesus and all that follows from it. Likewise, the answer makes it sound as if grace is something which accrues to a Christian's relation to God instead of being that very relation itself. Holiness *is* Christ's grace in us; it is not something we achieve.

437.   If Christian holiness is Christ's grace in us, then can there be any distinction between accepting Christian doctrine and growing in Christian life?

There is no distinction whatever. All that we have learned thus far about Christian doctrine has been but an explication of the graciousness of God as manifest in Christ Jesus. The Christian who understands and responds to it is leading a holy life.

PRAYER AND DETACHMENT

438.   If Christian holiness is Christ's grace in us, what are we to do to persevere in it?

Christian holiness is persevered in, first and always, by prayer. We merit continuance and growth in holiness by acknowledging in mind and heart God's graciousness to us in Christ. Thus, all Christian prayer begins with *praise* to God, our Father. It continues with *dedication* of ourselves to respond to his graciousness. It concludes with *petition* for what we need to live in God's grace as his beloved sons and daughters.

439.   After prayer, what must one do to live a life of persevering holiness?

"Good Teacher, what must I do to share in everlasting life?" (Lk 18:18). Jesus' response to this ageless question is simple: Keep God's commandments. And to this, Jesus adds: To be perfected in holiness, detach yourself from possessiveness in all its forms, be it self-will, self-gratification, or self-aggrandizement.

440.   But aren't the commandments a dead letter after the coming of Christ?

The Jewish law is a dead letter for Christians—so states the whole letter to the Galatians. But the spirit of that law is a different matter. Jesus announced that he came to perfect the Law, not to abolish it (Mt 5:17-19). If we would live in holiness, we must observe the commandments as Jesus lived and taught them. Putting it concretely, we must become disciples of Jesus in the Church.

441. And what of detachment, the perfection of Christian holiness?

There is no way of getting around the gospel demand for detachment. Self-will and sinfulness are equated in the gospel. The sinner is one who is a law unto himself. Christian holiness is perfected only as one shares in Christ's selfless obedience to the will of the heavenly Father.

442. How can Christian detachment be achieved?

One practices the natural excellence of character as they are graced by baptism and confirmation. These natural excellences are fairness, thoughtfulness, self-discipline, and perseverance. Of themselves, they are admirable traits of character. But practiced in order to live out the gospel, these excellences of character cannot but put an end to self-will, self-gratification, and self-aggrandizement.

THE MORAL EXCELLENCES

443.   Does this mean that there is a connection between following the gospel and good moral habits?

Indeed, there is. Good morals are the foundation and constant accompaniment of Christian holiness. A person cannot live the gospel of Jesus unless he has built up the stable and eduring moral character to which the gospel is addressed. Christian holiness does not exist in abstraction from good morals. (One might well ponder the Lord's parable of the sower in Mt 13:4-9 and 18-23.)

444.   What sort of character traits render a person unsuited to live the gospel?

St. Paul has done the description for us: "They are filled with every kind of wickedness: maliciousness, greed, ill will, envy, murder, bickering, deceit, craftiness. They are gossips and slanderers, they hate God, are insolent, haughty, boastful, ingenious in their wrongdoing and rebellious toward their parents. One sees in them men without conscience, without loyalty, without affection, without pity" (Rom 1:29-30).

445. Where did St. Paul get this list of vicious habits?

The list is pretty well borrowed from Greek Stoic philosophy. The Greek assessment of what makes for good and bad moral character was extremely sophisticated. A good bit of Stoicism enters into the New Testament and its wisdom is accepted by the Church.

446. What were the basic excellences of character in Greek ethics?

There are four basic excellences of character in Greek ethics:

a) good sense—the habit of taking thought before acting;
b) fairness—the habit of allowing for the rights of others;
c) self-discipline—the habit of emotional restraint;
d) courage—the habit of persevering in right action.

For Greek ethics, the utterly impetuous, me-first, emotionally unstable, and inconstant person was a human disaster. Throughout the ancient world, the four Greek values were commonly held as ideals of human excellence.

THE MORAL STANDARDS OF CHRISTIAN LIFE

447. In addition to good character, doesn't one also need good moral principles in order to live a life of Christian holiness?

Yes, one does. However, at the outset, good morals may have more to do with character-formation than with a profound understanding of good moral principles. The Greek ethicians already observed that one who wishes to become a good person needs first to be trained and habituated in the excellences of character before he can judge accurately about good and evil.

448. What are the moral standards of Christian life?

The moral standards of Christian life are God's commandments as taught and exemplified by Jesus. The commandments, followed in selfless obedience akin to that of Jesus, are not only the moral standards of the Christian life but are the royal road of Christian holiness. Our share in Jesus' loving obedience to the commands of the Father *is* Christian holiness.

Jesus is not the destination we reach by observing the commandments; he is the way (Jn 14:6) along which we learn to please the Father. There is no moment in Christian life when one, somehow, reaches a "higher path" than that of the commandments. (See the first letter of John for the strongest New Testament statement of this point.)

449. By the "commandments of God" do you mean the Ten Commandments?

Not literally and exclusively. But the basic values of Judaism, even as Jesus developed them, are always linked with one or another of the Ten Commandments. Thus, most expositions of Christian morality have used the Ten Commandments as the basic outline of moral values and disvalues. That will be our procedure two lessons hence.

450. How can one best learn the meaning of the commandments?

Practically speaking, the tradition of the Church in interpreting the meaning of the commandments is always a *safe* moral standard for Christian life. But it is not necessarily the loftiest standard. The Church's own moral sensitivity is always sharpened by both the saints and sinners it produces. The saints show the Church the yet-unfulfilled potentialities of the gospel. The sinners show the Church the shortcomings of its grasp of the gospel. Thus, an individual Christian may be called to demand more of himself than the Church demands.

451. But can't all the commandments be reduced to Jesus' great commandment to love God and love our neighbor?

Jesus' great commandment (Mt 22:33-40) is the property of Judaism as well as Christianity (Dt 6:5 and Lv 19:18). It certainly is true that all of the commandments are instances of what such love amounts to. But, from the mere command to love God and neighbor, we cannot clearly *deduce* all the commandments. Thus, Jesus' great commandment is more like a summing-up of Christian life rather than a substitute for specific moral standards.

452. If the commandment to love God and neighbor is not exactly original with Jesus, what is his great commandment?

"I give you a new commandment: Love one another. Such as my love has been for you, so must your love be for each other" (Jn 13:34). What is new is the *measure* of love which Jesus commands. It is Jesus' own selfless obedience to God's commandments which marks the morality of his disciples. There lies the unbreakable connection between Christian morality and Christian holiness. One who keeps the commandments according to this measure does a truly holy thing. He is following Christ in assurance that he is the way to the Father.

Chapter 19

SIN AND CONSCIENCE

CONSCIENCE

453. What is conscience?

Conscience is good judgment exercised upon the complexities of moral life. It is *not* a "still, small voice" mysteriously revealing what is right and wrong. Like any kind of good judgment, conscience grows and sharpens in its perceptions of what is right and wrong in a given situation.

454. What is the relation between conscience and morality?

Conscience is the individual's norm of morality. This simply means that a person cannot act against his best informed conscience if he wishes to do right. But this does not mean that his conscience makes the action right. He may, in fact, do wrong if he has failed to discern either the facts of the case or the moral principle involved.

455. But a person must follow his conscience, mustn't he?

If a person wishes to act rightly, he must follow his conscience because he cannot do anything else. It is the only judgment he has. But one's conscience is not an infallible guide which guarantees that what he actually does will be the right thing. It all depends on what sort of moral principles and what sort of moral habits enter into the judgment of conscience.

456. But this means that conscience, in order to be good, must measure up against some sort of moral standard, doesn't it?

Yes, a good conscience is a judgment upon the complexities of moral life according to a moral standard. A good action is meant to bring a value to bear upon a situation. A good conscience correctly estimates what value is called for in a given situation.

SIN

457. In the light of all this, what is sin?

Sin is the choice to act against one's informed conscience.

458. Thus, if a person had a poorly-informed conscience, he could sin without disobeying God's commandments?

Yes, he could. Even a poorly-informed conscience is the best judgment a person has. Thus, if a person had been taught that gambling or drinking were in themselves immoral, he would sin in choosing to do either. (For some practical advice on dealing with a person with a poorly-informed conscience, see Romans, chapters 14 and 15:1-6.)

459. Does it equally follow that a person could disobey God's commandments without sinning?

Yes, it is possible. A person with a poorly-informed conscience could disobey one of God's commandments without sinning. That is why moral standards must be *studied* and *understood*—one's conscience does not mysteriously reveal them.

Police walking the streets in the aftermath of a riot.

460. But aren't some things always sins, no matter what?

Some things are always *wrong*, no matter what. But a person with a poorly-informed conscience may judge inaccurately about them, especially if they are not immediately obvious. Thus, a person can do wrong without necessarily sinning.

461. What of one who does wrong and subsequently realizes it?

Someone who does wrong and subsequently realizes it has the moral obligation to atone for the consequences of his wrongdoing to the extent that he can. If he chooses not to, he sins.

462. What of someone who is not sure that his past wrongdoing was really sinful?

One who is conducting an "examination of conscience" should ask himself: (a) whether, at the time of the wrongdoing, he clearly apprehended the moral principle at stake in all its seriousness; (b) whether, at the time of the wrongdoing, he purposely chose to disregard his judgment as to what was right in the light of the moral principle he apprehended.

If the answer to either or both questions is negative, he has not sinned. If the outcome of his examination is genuine uncertainty on either or both questions, he has not sinned. His own conscience testifies as to uncertainty about the clear-cut choice which is sin.

MORTAL AND VENIAL SIN

463. Does the Bible add any new notion to sin beyond just not following one's informed conscience?

Yes. Genuine sin in the Bible is always described as a *rebellion* against God. The sinner casts away God's graciousness in Christ and chooses to be a law unto himself.

464. But surely not everything sinful is also a rebellion against God?

Obviously not. The Bible speaks of understandable and forgivable offenses which even the righteous commit (see 1 Jn

5:16-17; Jas 3:2). From this, Christian moralists evolved the distinction between mortal and venial sin.

465.   What is the distinction between mortal and venial sin?

Looking at the distinction from one angle, it is a difference of *magnitude*. Mortal sin is a choice to nullify God's commandment. Venial sin is a choice to stop short in obedience to God's commandment. Mortal sin breaks the relation of grace; venial sin weakens the relation of grace.

466.   Could you give an example of a mortal and a venial sin?

One who chooses to tell a lie which completely ruins someone's reputation commits mortal sin because he shows utter contempt for the commandment not to bear false witness. One who indulges willingly in petty gossip commits venial sin because he allows his tongue to run on knowing that no one will take it too seriously.

467.   Is it just "how much" wrong that is done which makes the distinction between mortal and venial sin?

Such a distinction is surely not adequate. It makes it sound as if venial sin is what one can get away with and mortal sin is what one cannot get away with. A more adequate distinction is obviously needed.

468.   What is the deepest distinction between mortal and venial sin?

The deepest distinction between mortal and venial sin lies in the *imperfection* of human character as it conditions our freedom of choice. There simply are universal human faults in ourselves and others. As we learn of their existence, we tolerate them even though they occasion a fair amount of wrongdoing. For instance, we simply do not believe everything we hear about others because we know of our own propensity for gossip. Thus, venial sin does little harm *because we allow for it.*

Mortal sin, on the other hand, is a choice to do evil inexplicable in the light of ordinary human frailties, blameworthy as they may be.

469. If mortal sin is a choice to do evil inexplicable in the light of ordinary human frailties, doesn't it follow that it is practically impossible for someone to commit mortal sin without a previous history of venial sin?

Arguing whether one could commit mortal sin "on the first try" is a rather unpleasant exercise in abstract logic. Anything is possible, and a human being could freely alter his whole life by a single choice.

But, practically speaking, persons have histories and seldom act outside of them. A previous history of venial sin seems to be the context which gives some sort of intelligibility to the ultimately inexplicable choice to do grave moral wrong. Thus, one would tend to judge that it is practically impossible to commit mortal sin by one, single decision unrelated to a person's whole moral life.

470. Could someone commit venial sin after venial sin and still be in the grace of God?

If one is speaking of human actions taken out of any context, one could commit innumerable venial sins and still be in God's grace. But, in fact, a person does not sin out of any context. Someone who is willing to allow for all sorts of venial sins is also choosing to tolerate genuine faults in his character. And that, in the long run, is immoral.

471. Could something which, in itself, is a venial sin become a mortal sin for a given person?

Yes, it could. For instance, an act of petty dishonesty could become a test-case for an individual as to the whole future of his life. If such a consequence is foreseen, mortal sin could ensue.

472. Could something which, in itself, is a venial sin become a mortal sin because of circumstances?

Yes, it could. For example, an ordinarily petty deception if practiced on a child or a simple person, could lead to a serious misapprehension of what is really true. If such a consequence is foreseen and chosen, mortal sin could ensue.

473.   Could something which, in itself, is a mortal sin become a venial sin because of circumstances?

Yes, it could. Blameless ignorance or overpowering emotion or inveterate habit can diminish or even completely remove the guilt of mortal sin. Sin is a *choice,* and a choice requires that one be conscious of alternatives.

474.   Can circumstances also aggravate the guilt of mortal and venial sin?

Yes, they can. If someone chooses to avoid finding out what he needs to know in order to make a moral decision, he aggravates his guilt. If someone decides to work up his emotions in order to justify an immoral decision, he aggravates his guilt. If someone allows free rein to an immoral habit, he aggravates the guilt of his actions.

OCCASIONS OF SIN

475.   What is an occasion of sin?

An occasion of sin is a set of circumstances which impel a person toward sin. One who freely and knowingly puts himself in an *avoidable* occasion of sin is already guilty of some sin, depending upon how impelling he foreknows the circumstances to be.

476.   Can someone avoid all occasions of sin?

A person cannot and need not avoid all occasions of sin. Some are built into his daily round of duties; some are built into life itself. The moral obligation is to deal rightly with these circumstances and not to become scrupulous about the effect they have on our feelings.

Chapter 20

THE TEN COMMANDMENTS

HOW TO UNDERSTAND THE COMMANDMENTS

477. Where are the Ten Commandments found in the Bible?

The Ten Commandments are found in two places in the Bible: Exodus 20:1-17 and Deuteronomy 5:6-21.

478. What is the difference between the Catholic and Protestant numbering of the Ten Commandments?

The "Catholic" commandments are one number previous to the "Protestant" commandments, e.g., the Catholic second commandment is the Protestant third commandment. Protestants, generally, have followed the tradition which makes the prohibition against graven images a second commandment, separate from the first commandment to worship God alone.

479. How can one best understand the Ten Commandments in the spirit of Jesus?

The best way to understand the Ten Commandments in the spirit of Jesus is to think of each commandment as *commanding* something and *commending* something. Each commandment speaks of actions to be done or avoided. Each commandment also recommends a moral value which is to be prized in life. This is how Jesus treats the commandments in the sermon on the mount (Mt 5:20-48).

480.   Is there any official interpretation by the Church of exactly everything which the Ten Commandments forbid?

No, there is no such thing. Church authorities are not in possession of a "black book" of sins which they consult upon inquiry. Instances of right and wrong cannot be *deduced* from the Ten Commandments. Instances of right and wrong just happen and one's conscience *judges* them in the light of the Commandments. Sometimes, one needs the skill of a moral theologian to judge very complex instances.

481.   Doesn't the Church have any "official" list of sins?

No, it does not. Throughout its long history, the Church has judged that certain sorts of behavior are clearly wrong, or rash, or dangerous. Obviously, though, these judgments do not and cannot exhaust the possibilities of human sinfulness. Morality is a matter of good judgment in the light of good moral principles. Not even the Church can foresee every possible case of evil which will occur nor can it foresee all possible implications of the moral teachings of Jesus.

482.   So this lesson on the Ten Commandments is not a definitive and final summary of Christian morality?

No lesson on the Ten Commandments can be such a summary. This lesson suggests lines along which the Ten Commandments can be understood and lines of self-examination along which the Ten Commandments can be applied to types of human behavior.

*SELF-EXAMINATION IN THE LIGHT OF
EACH COMMANDMENT*

483.   The First Commandment: "I am the Lord, your God; you shall not have strange gods before me."

The First Commandment tells us that there is nothing we need to fear and nothing we ought to worship except God, our heavenly Father, as revealed in Christ. Everything in the universe is but our fellow-creature. Thus, no natural or human power can compel our total allegiance nor may we give it such allegiance.

484. How may one examine himself in the light of the First Commandment?

Self-examination in the light of the First Commandment may well center around what we truly idolize. Our possessions, our status, our work, etc. can all be truly the things we would not give up for anything in the world. Our religion, on the contrary, may be something we are perfectly willing to compromise if it comes into genuine conflict with what we hold dearest.

485. The Second Commandment: "You shall not take the name of the Lord, your God, in vain."

The Second Commandment tells us that God will not tolerate being treated like anything else than what he truly is: our loving, heavenly Father. All his divinity is engaged in a loving and sharing relation with his beloved sons and daughters in Christ. We sin against the Commandment by treating God as something he is not—by making him an indulgent Santa Claus or a heavenly policeman. If we so invoke his name to accomplish our will, we do no honor to his name.

486. How may one examine himself in the light of the Second Commandment?

Self-examination in the light of the Second Commandment may well center around how we think and speak of God. The things we think that God should be responsible for and the things we think that God should do for us reveal our reverence or irreverence toward him. The height of irreverence is to call upon his name or his power to accomplish some unworthy or unholy purpose of our own.

487. The Third Commandment: "Remember to keep holy the Sabbath day."

The Third Commandment tells us that total preoccupation with ourselves and our occupations will damn us. There must be space in our lives for times of worship and moments of thought about God and what God has called us to become in Christ. This age and this world cannot be our masters because our lives open out onto an age and a world yet to come.

488.   How may one examine himself in the light of the Third Commandment?

Self-examination in the light of the Third Commandment may well center around the sincerity of our search for holiness. What we have time for and what we make time for reveals what we think is important or unimportant in life. If we discover that worship, prayer, reflection, and repentance are things we never get around to, our response to God's graciousness in Christ is nil.

489.   The Fourth Commandment: "Honor your father and mother."

The Fourth Commandment reminds us that no human is self-sufficient. We sin against this commandment by ingratitude in all its forms, by taking all our human relationships for granted. Insensitivity to the needs of those who depend on us and insensitivity to the concerns of those upon whom we depend make it impossible for any human relationship to survive.

The family constitutes the basic unit of human ties.

490. How may one examine himself in the light of the Fourth Commandment?

Self-examination in the light of the Fourth Commandment may well center around whom we truly care about. What we are available for and what we make available for those who look to us for care reveals how sensitive we are to human ties. If our time, our interests, our plans, etc. are first and foremost self-centered, we have no human ties worth mentioning, especially with those for whom we must provide.

491. The Fifth Commandment: "You shall not kill."

The Fifth Commandment tells us that no individual may judge a human life, including his own, as so worthless that it may be deliberately destroyed or harmed. We sin against this commandment by determining when there is no purpose nor use to a life and acting accordingly. Our act may not be literally a murder of the body; there are also many subtle ways of killing a person's spirit.

492. How may one examine himself in the light of the Fifth Commandment?

Self-examination in the light of the Fifth Commandment may well center around our prejudices, our intolerances, and our lack of respect for those from whom we differ. One who feels that someone does not deserve a chance at the goods of life or, even worse, that "they" just clutter up the earth, reveals the arrogance which underlies all violence.

493. The Sixth Commandment: "You shall not commit adultery."

The Sixth Commandment tells us that human sexuality and the commitment of marriage are inseparable. We cannot share bodies without sharing lives. We sin against this commandment by merely using our sexuality without intending to give our love as well. Seduction is a lie-in-act about love and the seriousness of love. Follow the lie to its roots and you will discover someone who loves the pleasures of love with utter disregard for whom or what they involve.

494.   How may one examine himself in the light of the Sixth Commandment?

Self-examination in the light of the Sixth Commandment may well center around all our urges for self-gratification and how heedless we are of their consequences. When self-gratification becomes a need before which all restraint falls, we have allowed ourselves to be corrupted. Then it really doesn't matter what the object of our heedless pursuit may be.

495.   The Seventh Commandment: "You shall not steal."

The Seventh Commandment reminds us that human beings are dependent upon the world around them for security. God commands that we do not take from another or prevent another from obtaining the resources which fairly belong to him. We sin against this commandment by injustice in all its forms, including economic injustice. The goods of this world must be fairly distributed and fairly available for the well-being of all humankind, including the generations yet to come.

496.   How may one examine himself in the light of the Seventh Commandment?

Self-examination in the light of the Seventh Commandment may well center around our very sense of justice. What we owe to others is not always measured by money. We all seem to have a good idea of what we need, in fairness, for our well-being. But something seems to blunt that same sense of fairness when the well-being of others is concerned. Somehow, profiting from another is not as bad as when that other person manages to profit from us.

497.   The Eighth Commandment: "You shall not bear false witness."

The Eighth Commandment reminds us that human beings rely on each other's word and performance for their well-being. We sin against this commandment not only when we speak falsely against each other but also when we fail to live up to our obligations. Human society cannot survive when individuals have to cope with fraud, deception, nonperformance, and general dishonesty in every one of their dealings with their fellowman.

498. How may one examine himself in the light of the Eighth Commandment?

Self-examination in the light of the Eighth Commandment may well center around our personal honesty and dependability. What is it, truly, that we would never lie or cheat to accomplish?

499. The Ninth Commandment: "You shall not covet your neighbor's wife."

The Ninth Commandment tells us that our attitude toward human love must be a truly internal reverence. God reminds us that certain things are genuinely unthinkable. There must be a divine intolerance in our lives for whatever would dishonor a pledge of love once given.

500. How may one examine himself in the light of the Ninth Commandment?

Self-examination in the light of the Ninth Commandment may well center around the lengths we would be willing to go in order to achieve our own gratification. Just what plans would we entertain or what would we be willing to destroy in order that we might gain someone's love?

501. The Tenth Commandment: "You shall not covet your neighbor's goods."

The Tenth Commandment reminds us that no amount of law is going to ensure justice if there is no internal reverence for justice in us. Society is a precarious thing; it depends upon human good will. We sin against this commandment by disrespect or contempt for the institutions which men have created in order to protect their rights. The will-to-justice embraces not only property, but human and political rights as well.

502. How may one examine himself in the light of the Tenth Commandment?

Self-examination in the light of the Tenth Commandment may well center around the lengths to which we would be willing to go in order to achieve our own security. What amount of oppression would we be willing to tolerate in the lives of others in order that our own wealth, our own status, and our own power might be secured?

Chapter 21

GOD'S JUDGMENT

503. Where do the gospels put Jesus' teaching on the end of the world?

The synoptic gospels associate Jesus' teaching on the end of the world with the final journey to Jerusalem (Mt 19—25; Mk 11—13; Lk 19—21). St. John's gospel presents all of Jesus' deeds and teachings as a judgment on unbelievers.

504. How literally are we to take Jesus' description of the events which will occur at the end of time?

Probably not literally at all. They are borrowed from a stock set of apocalyptic images. The same holds true for the end-time as described in the book of Revelation. Apocalyptic literature is imaginative vision, not literal prediction.

505. Are Jesus' parables on the judgment actual descriptions of an event which will take place at the end of the world?

Jesus' parables on the judgment have no particular time-reference at all. That is, these parables do not seem to describe any specific, concrete event such as Christian artists picture as the "Last Judgment." Even the detailed picture of the coming of the Son of Man in the synoptic gospels is a stock apocalyptic image (see Dn 7:13-14).

506. What are we to make of this odd haziness in Jesus' teaching on the end of the world?

The odd haziness is due to us, not to Jesus. Christian imagination has constructed a scenario of happenings which obscures the actual teaching of Jesus.

507. What is the actual teaching of Jesus on the end of the world?

Jesus' actual teaching is quite plain in the gospels. In proclaiming the kingdom of heaven, Jesus is *equally* proclaiming the end of the world. The end-time begins with him and all the events of the end-time are in the process of happening ever since.

508. What are the events of the end-time?

Christian imagination has constructed the scenario: death, judgment, heaven or hell. Since this scenario has become so embedded in Christian imagination, one can use it as a convenient device to present Jesus' teaching on the end of the world. But each item in the scenario needs correction and amplification.

DEATH AND CHRISTIAN HOPE

509. What does my death have to do with the end of the world?

On the face of it, one's own death and personal judgment have nothing in particular to do with the end of the world. Even Jesus' many parables about stewardship have nothing in them especially directed toward the end-time. The parables merely make the point, common to many religions, that each of us will have to give an account of our lives to a divine judge.

510. Does a Christian's death and personal judgment have anything to do with the end of the world?

A Christian's death and personal judgment can have something to do with the end of the world. A Christian's living and dying are a share in the dying and rising of Jesus (Rom 6:3-9).

"Aware of the bonds linking the whole Mystical Body . . ., the pilgrim Church from the very first ages . . . has cultivated with great piety the memory of the dead" (Vat. II: The Church, no. 50).

If Jesus' dying and rising are what inaugurate the end-time, then a Christian living out his baptismal calling is already in the end-time. His living and dying in awareness of his baptismal grace helps *bring on* the end of this sinful world. Or, if the Christian lives and dies unresponsive to his baptismal calling, he can delay the advent of the world-to-come.

511. Saying that a Christian's living and dying in awareness of his baptismal grace can bring on the end of this sinful world sounds like sheer poetry. What proves that it is true?

The demands of Christian discipleship are surely not of *this* world. In fact, the demands which Christ makes would be sheer nonsense if this world were to last forever. Forgiving *all* wrongs, for instance, is beyond the bounds of our natural human tolerance. The forgiving Christian is living out a totally new relationship between human beings. And that relationship is surely not at all appropriate to this sinful world.

512. But perhaps the demands of Christian discipleship are simply lofty ideals and have nothing at all to do with the world-to-come. What proves that a Christian's faithfulness to the end is going to make anything happen?

Christianity is anything but a religion of sheer idealism. A Christian lives in genuine *hope* in the power of the risen

Jesus, not in some quixotic reaction against things-as-they-are. Christian hope has concrete grounds for its expectation of what-is-to-come. For one of the earliest statements of the grounds of Christian hope, see the eighth chapter of Romans.

513. Could it be said that a Christian's whole life is a sort of dying to this world and living in hope of the world-to-come?

The Lord himself said it: "If a man wishes to come after me, he must deny his very self, take up his cross, and begin to follow in my footsteps. Whoever would save his life will lose it, but whoever loses his life for my sake will find it" (Mt 16:24-25, compare Jn 12:25-26).

514. Does this mean that a Christian's actual, physical death is given a new meaning because he lives in hope?

The actual death of one who has lived out his baptismal calling is at the same time, the beginning of his resurrection. Death does not put an end to a Christian; he puts an end to death. His death helps bring on the end-time. "When the corruptible frame takes on incorruptibility and the mortal immortality, then will the saying of Scripture be fulfilled: 'Death is swallowed up in victory.' 'O death, where is your victory? O death, where is your sting?' " (1 Cor 15:54-55).

515. Is dying in Christian hope the same as Christian resignation in the face of death?

There is no such thing as Christian resignation in the face of death. Even Jesus prayed to be delivered from death (Lk 22:41-44). Death is a factor in a *sinful* world, not some inevitable feature in the scheme of things. It is un-Christian to endure suffering and death except in the same hope with which Jesus endured them. Just as Jesus lived in utter confidence that his heavenly Father would not fail him, so the Christian lives and dies in the confidence that his suffering and dying will hasten the end of suffering and death.

THE "HERE" AND THE "HEREAFTER"

516.   If all the events of the end-time are already in the process of happening, does that mean that judgment, heaven, and hell are already in the process of happening?

Yes, judgment, heaven, and hell are, to some extent, "here" as well as "hereafter." A Christian cannot make a neat distinction between this world and the world-to-come. This world is precisely what is evolving into the world-to-come under the power of the risen savior. (See Rom 8.)

517.   Isn't "here" the physical world and "hereafter" some sort of spiritual world?

This distinction is completely foreign to Christianity. The correct distinction is between this world and the world-to-come. The "hereafter" is being brought into existence precisely from what is "here." Thus, the hereafter is *not yet* in full existence.

HEAVEN AND HELL NOW AND AS THEY WILL BE

518.   But if the hereafter is not yet in full existence, haven't those who have died been already judged and rewarded or punished?

As one might suspect, fidelity to the New Testament notion that the hereafter is not yet in full existence led to quite a bit of confusion about the status of those who have already died (see 1 Thes 4:13-18 for the earliest example). Church tradition did not receive its definitive form until 1336, when the apostolic constitution *Benedictus Deus* of Benedict XII stated Catholic belief in an immediate judgment, reward, or punishment of those who have died.

519.   If the hereafter is not yet in full existence, what are things like now for those who have died?

Perhaps the best way to arrive at a satisfactory description of the state of the departed is to *subtract* features which belong only to the world-to-come and see what remains. The one thing which is surely "not yet" is the kingdom of God. Bringing the kingdom of God into existence is Christ's final act of Lordship. Its accomplishment is the general resurrection.

At that moment, it becomes supremely evident that Christ *is* Lord. At that moment, too, it becomes supremely evident that belief or unbelief in his Lordship is what was decisive in human history. The coming-into-being of the kingdom of God *is* the "last judgment" on sin for all to read. (See 1 Cor 15:20-28.)

520. What is missing for those saved or damned until the kingdom of God appears?

Neither the saved nor the damned yet form a *society* whose whole way of life shows that Christ is Lord.

521. Does this mean that salvation or damnation are incomplete for those who have died?

It all depends on what one means by "incomplete." One's personal reward or punishment, depending upon one's personal belief or unbelief in God's saving power in Christ, are clearly experienced by those who have died—allowing, of course, for a period of purgation for those who have consequences of repented sin for which to atone. The reward is a personal experience of the inner delight of the Persons of the Trinity in their communion in the one divinity, i.e., eternal life. The punishment is everlasting exclusion from eternal life and the torment(s) of spirit consequent upon it.

522. What is so incomplete about heaven and hell as they have just been described?

What is incomplete, what is the great *mysterion*, is just precisely what expansion or transformation of the human person will occur at the general resurrection. The resurrection is not a mere resuscitation of humankind. Rather, those who rise to eternal life will, one suspects, have a whole range of capacities, bodily and mental, added to their persons. On the other hand, those who rise to damnation, will have their human capacities brutalized in physical counterpart to their moral state.

523. Aren't those who are in heaven as rewarded as they can be and those in hell as punished as they can be?

They are as rewarded or punished as they have the *capacity* to be. But they, like us, look forward to what will happen at the advent of the kingdom of God. The saved await its coming with joy; the damned with fear.

524. Do we actually know of persons saved and damned?

"Saved" and "damned" are abstract categories. Aside from the obvious instances of the saints, we dare not presume who is saved. Nor, aside from the obvious instance of Satan, dare we presume who may be damned.

525. Wouldn't one prefer to think that no human person is or even could be damned to everlasting punishment?

Indeed, the thought of everlasting punishment is simply beyond our human capacities. But we dare not discount the possibility. The issue of belief or unbelief in God's saving power in Christ is not just one among many choices a person must make in life. It is *the* choice determining a person's stance toward life itself. One who chooses unbelief has chosen what he will be. Really, God sends no one to hell; the unbeliever chooses hell in choosing unbelief.

526. If the unbeliever chooses hell in choosing unbelief, aren't you saying that judgment, reward, or punishment are already present in his life?

Yes, they are *present* factors in life. The end-time and the world-to-come are in the process of happening in our midst. The moral is simple: Repentance from sin and the pursuit of Christian holiness have visible consequences, as do their opposites. The society of the saved and the society of the damned are being formed. No one can claim that he could not discern the characteristics of each. Christ's timeless parables on judgment point them out to us, and there is no excuse for failing to comprehend them.

527. When the kingdom of God arrives, what will heaven and hell be like?

It will be "eternal life" versus "eternal death." The community of the saved, risen to transformed existence, will forever share in their Lord's very experience of the Father's everlasting love in the Holy Spirit. From this experience, the saved will create a style of life and self-expression (art? work? leisure?) giving everlasting glory to the Father and everlasting joy to each and all.

The community of the damned, brutalized by infidelity, will forever seek a way to live together in infidelity. Like Satan, they will forever fail to create anything of value or beauty or meaning. Their human resources are dead and they have lost the power to evoke any response from any creature, their fellows included.

"I heard a loud voice from the throne cry out: 'This is God's dwelling among men. He shall dwell with them and they shall be his people and he shall be their God who is always with them. He shall wipe every tear from their eyes, and there shall be no more death or mourning, crying out or pain, for the former world has passed away' " (Rev 21:3-4).

APPENDIX

THE TEN COMMANDMENTS OF GOD

1. I, the Lord, am your God. You shall not have other gods besides me.
2. You shall not take the name of the Lord, your God, in vain.
3. Remember to keep holy the sabbath day.
4. Honor your father and your mother.
5. You shall not kill.
6. You shall not commit adultery.
7. You shall not steal.
8. You shall not bear false witness against your neighbor.
9. You shall not covet your neighbor's wife.
10. You shall not covet anything that belongs to your neighbor.

DUTIES OF CATHOLICS

1. To keep holy the day of the Lord's Resurrection: to worship God by participating in Mass every Sunday and Holy Day of Obligation:* to avoid those activities that would hinder renewal of soul and body, e.g., needless work and business activities, unnecessary shopping, etc.
2. To lead a sacramental life: to receive Holy Communion frequently and the Sacrament of Penance
   —minimally, to receive the Sacrament of Penance at least once a year (annual confession is obligatory only if serious sin is involved);*
   —minimally, to receive Holy Communion at least once a year, between the First Sunday of Lent and Trinity Sunday.*

Note:
   (Duties traditionally mentioned as Precepts of the Church are marked with an asterisk)
   The traditionally listed chief Precepts of the Church are the following six:
   1. To assist at Mass on all Sundays and holy days of obligation.
   2. To fast and abstain on the days appointed.
   3. To confess our sins at least once a year.
   4. To receive Holy Communion during the Easter time.
   5. To contribute to the support of the Church.
   6. To observe the laws of the Church concerning marriage.

3. To study Catholic teaching in preparation for the Sacrament of Confirmation, to be confirmed, and then to continue to study and advance the cause of Christ.
4. To observe the marriage laws of the Church:* to give religious training (by example and word) to one's children; to use parish schools and religious education programs.
5. To strengthen and support the Church:* one's own parish community and parish priests; the worldwide Church and the Holy Father.
6. To do penance, including abstaining from meat and fasting from food on the appointed days.*
7. To join in the missionary spirit and apostolate of the Church.

ESSENTIAL PRAYERS

Recommended by the National Conference
of Catholic Bishops

SIGN OF THE CROSS

In the name of the Father, and of the Son, and of the Holy Spirit. Amen.

THE LORD'S PRAYER

Our Father, who art in heaven, hallowed by Thy name; Thy kingdom come; Thy will be done on earth as it is in heaven. Give us this day our daily bread; and forgive us our trespasses as we forgive those who trespass against us; and lead us not into temptation, but deliver us from evil. Amen.

HAIL MARY

Hail Mary, full of grace! the Lord is with you; blessed are you among women, and blessed is the fruit of your womb, Jesus. Holy Mary, Mother of God, pray for us sinners, now and at the hour of our death. Amen.

DOXOLOGY

Glory be to the Father, and to the Son, and to the Holy Spirit. As it was in the beginning, is now, and ever shall be, world without end. Amen.

THE APOSTLES' CREED

I believe in God the Father Almighty, Creator of heaven and earth; and in Jesus Christ, His only Son, our Lord; Who was conceived by the Holy Spirit, born of the Virgin Mary; suffered under Pontius Pilate, was crucified, died, and was buried; He descended into hell; the third day He rose again from the dead; He ascended into heaven and sits at the right hand of God the Father Almighty; from thence He shall come to judge the living and the dead. I believe in the Holy Spirit; the Holy Catholic Church; the Communion of Saints; the forgiveness of sins; the resurrection of the body; and life everlasting. Amen.

ACT OF CONTRITION

O my God, I am heartily sorry for having offended You, and I detest all my sins, because of Your just punishments, but most of all because they offend You, my God, Who are all good and deserving of all my love. I firmly resolve, with the help of Your grace, to sin no more and to avoid the near occasions of sin.

ACT OF FAITH

O my God, I firmly believe all the truths that the holy Catholic Church believes and teaches; I believe these truths, O Lord, because You, the infallible Truth, have revealed them to her: in this faith I am resolved to live and die. Amen.

ACT OF HOPE

O my God, trusting in Your promises, and because You are faithful, powerful and merciful, I hope, through the merits of Jesus Christ, for the pardon of my sins, final perseverance, and the blessed glory of heaven. Amen.

ACT OF CHARITY

O my God, because You are infinite Goodness and worthy of infinite love, I love You with my whole heart above all things, and for love of You, I love my fellow-men as myself. Amen.

HAIL, HOLY QUEEN

Hail, holy Queen, Mother of mercy; hail our life, our sweetness, and our hope. To you do we cry, poor banished children of Eve. To you do we send up our sighs, mourning and weeping in this valley of tears. Turn then, most gracious Advocate, your eyes of mercy toward us. And after this our exile show unto us the blessed fruit of your womb, Jesus, O clement, O loving, O sweet Virgin Mary.

THE MYSTERIES OF THE ROSARY

The Joyful Mysteries

1. The Annunciation of the Archangel Gabriel to the Virgin Mary.
2. The Visitation of the Virgin Mary to the Parents of St. John the Baptist.
3. The Birth of Our Lord at Bethlehem.
4. The Presentation of Our Lord in the Temple.
5. The Finding of Our Lord in the Temple.

The Sorrowful Mysteries

1. The Agony of Our Lord in the Garden of Gethsemane.
2. The Scourging of Our Lord at the Pillar.
3. The Crowning of Our Lord with Thorns.
4. The Carrying of the Cross by Our Lord to Calvary.
5. The Crucifixion and Death of Our Lord.

The Glorious Mysteries

1. The Resurrection of Our Lord from the dead.
2. The Ascension of Our Lord into Heaven.
3. The Descent of the Holy Spirit upon the Disciples.
4. The Assumption of Our Blessed Lady into Heaven.
5. The Coronation of Our Blessed Lady as Queen of Heaven and Earth.

EXCERPTS FROM THE "NATIONAL CATECHETICAL DIRECTORY"

*Showing How the "People's Catechism" Accords
with This Official Document of the Church*

(Chapter Headings of this Catechism are in Bold type)

Foreword: "The content of adult catechesis is as comprehensive and diverse as the Church's mission." (185)

1. The God of the Bible: ". . . revelation designates that communication of God which is in no way deserved by us, for it has as its aim our participation in the life of the Trinity, a share in the divine life itself." (49)

2. **God and Man:** "The term 'biblical signs' refers to the varied and wonderful ways, recorded in scripture, by which God reveals Himself. Among the chief signs, to be emphasized in all catechesis, are: the creation account, which culminates in the establishment of God's kingdom; the covenant made by God with Abraham and his descendants. . . ." (43)

3. **The Story of Salvation:** "God spoke to His people through judges and kings, priests and prophets, sages and biblical writers. . . . He inspired authors to record the words and deeds of revelation for the benefit of future generations, and to bring forth from the community the Old Testament accounts which best express His love." (52)

4. The Life of Jesus: "God's revelation reached its supreme expression in the incarnation, life, death, burial, and resurrection of Jesus Christ, by the power of the Spirit. Jesus inaugurated God's kingdom among human beings." (53)

5. Jesus Christ, the Redeemer: "By His life, death, and resurrection He redeemed humankind from slavery to sin and the devil. Truly risen, the Lord is the unfailing source of life and of the outpouring of the Holy Spirit upon the human race." (90)

6. Jesus Christ, the Lord: "As a mystery, the Church cannot be totally understood or fully defined. Its nature and mission are best captured in scriptural parables and images. . . ." (63)

7. The Church and the World: "The Church . . . is called to be a sign of God's kingdom already in our midst. It is called to serve the kingdom and to advance it among all peoples of the world." (67)

8. The Divided Churches: "Certain signs or marks identify this community of faith. . . . They are gifts bestowed upon the Church by the Lord—but gifts which the Church must also strive to realize more fully in its life." (72)   )

9. Interchurch Cooperation: "Catechesis should also be sensitive in dealing with the separated churches and ecclesial communities of the West, many of which share much in common with Catholic tradition. The numerous bilateral studies and proposed agreements should be suitably presented." (76)

10. Church Organization: "The clergy serve the Church through authentic Christian teaching, sacramental ministry, and direction in various organizations and activities for God's kingdom. Of special importance for unity of faith are the Church's official teachings on matters of faith and morals authoritatively promulgated by the pope and bishops." (69)

11. The Church at Worship: "The Eucharist is a memorial of the Lord's passion, death, and resurrection. . . . Through, with, and in the Church, Christ's sacrifice on the cross and the victory of His resurrection become present in every celebration. . . . In the Eucharist, Christ the Lord nourishes Christians, not only with His word but especially with His body and blood, effecting a transformation which impels them toward greater love of God and neighbor." (120)

12. The Sacraments: "The sacraments, symbolic actions which effect what they symbolize, celebrate the coming of the Spirit at special moments in the life of the community of faith and its members and express the Church's faith and interaction with Christ." (114)

13. Sacraments of Initiation: "Christian initiation is celebrated in Baptism, Confirmation or Chrismation, and Eucharist. Through these visible actions a person is incorporated into the Church and shares its mission in the world." (115)

14. Sacraments of Crisis: "We are incorporated into Christ's body, the Church, through the Sacraments of Initiation. When we have been weakened by sin or sickness, we are healed and strengthened within that body, through the sacraments of Reconciliation and Anointing of the Sick." (123)

15. Sacraments of Vocation: "Every Christian's ultimate commitment is to love and serve God revealed in Jesus Christ present in His Church. But individual Christians are called to live out this commitment in various ways. . . . The sacraments of Matrimony and Holy Orders celebrate these callings, and sanctify and strengthen those who commit themselves to them." (129)

16. Divorce and Remarriage: "Concern for those who have suffered the trauma of divorce should be integral to the Catholic community. . . . Catechesis on the Church's teaching concerning the consequences of remarriage after divorce is not only necessary but will be supportive for the divorced." (131)

17. Mary—Mother and Disciple: "Singularly blessed, Mary speaks significantly to our lives and needs in the sinlessness of her total love. Following venerable Christian tradition . . . the Church recognizes her as loving mother, its 'model and excellent exemplar in faith and charity.' " (106)

18. Christian Holiness: "God reveals to us in Jesus who we are and how we are to live. It is His plan that we freely respond, making concrete in the particular circumstances of our lives what the call to holiness and the commandment of love require of us." (101)

19. Sin and Conscience: "We live in good faith if we act in accord with conscience. Nevertheless moral decisons still require much effort. Decisions of conscience must be based upon prayer, study, consultation, and understanding of the teachings of the Church." (103)

20. The Ten Commandments: "The obligations which flow from love of God and human beings should be taught in a specific, practical way. . . . The specifics of morality should be taught in the light of the Ten Commandments, the Sermon on the Mount, especially the beatitudes, and Christ's discourse at the Last Supper." (105)

21. God's Judgment: "During their earthly lives Christians look forward to final union with God in heaven. They long for Christ's coming. . . . The final realities will come about only when Christ returns with power to bring history to its appointed end. Then, as judge of the living and the dead, He will hand over His people to the Father. Only then will the Church reach perfection." (110)

TOPICAL INDEX

OTHER OUTSTANDING CATHOLIC BOOKS

HOLY BIBLE—Saint Joseph Edition of the completely modern translation called the **New American Bible**. Printed in large type with helpful Notes and Maps, Photographs, Family Record Pages and Bible Dictionary. **Ask for No. 611.**

ST. JOSEPH SUNDAY MISSAL and HYMNAL—Complete and permanent Edition with all Official texts for Sundays and Holydays. Includes the **New American Bible** of the Readings for Years **A, B,** and **C,** with Mass introductions and helpful explanations. People's responses clearly indicated in heavy print. 1536 pages 167 popular Hymns. **Ask for No. 820.**

ST. JOSEPH WEEKDAY MISSAL (Vol. I & II)—All the Mass texts needed for weekdays. Indispensable aid for all who celebrate and participate at daily Mass. **Ask for Nos. 920 & 921.**

NEW TESTAMENT—St. Joseph Edition of the New American Bible Version. Large easy-to-ready type, with helpful Notes and Maps, Photographs, Background to the New Testament, and Handy Study Guide. 432 pages. **Ask for No. 311.**

Pocket Edition — legible type, illus. 672 pages. **Ask for No. 630.**

ST. JOSEPH COMMENTARY ON THE SUNDAY READINGS — By Achille Degeest, O.F.M. Concise commentaries for the Sunday Mass Readings in a clear and non-technical manner that gives the essential message of the Church. It will be of great help to all Catholics. Separate volumes for each Year.
Ask for No. 341 (Year A), No. 342 (Year B), No. 343 (Year C).

ST. JOSEPH BIBLE CATECHISM — By Rev. John Kersten, S.V.D. The History of Salvation presented through the BIBLE and the LITURGY. A new Complete Kerygmatic approach. Ideal for High Schools and CCD classes, Bible Readings, Study Helps. Illustrated. **Ask for No. 245**

EVERY DAY WE PRAISE YOU—By Rev. V. Hoagland, C.P., and Sister M. Skelly, S.C. A beautiful new book of prayers and devotions for the year. It includes prayers for the Blessed Sacrament, Penance Rite, Seasons of the Year, and Morning and Evening Prayer from the first Week of the Psalter, taken from the official "Liturgy of the Hours." **— Ask for No. 315**

BIBLE MEDITATIONS FOR EVERY DAY—By John Kersten, S.V.D. Excellent aid for daily meditation. A Scripture passage and a short introduction are given for every day of the year.
— Ask for No. 277

Wherever Catholic Books are Sold